Walter and Lisetta

Living, Loving, Learning

by

Fauneil Fremont

ISBN: 978-1-965951-27-9 (sc)

Seraphim Global Media LLC
155 Willowbrook Blvd Ste 110 Wayne, NJ 07470
+1 888-347-1877
fullfillment@seraphimgml.com

In honor of

Walter and Lisetta

and Minnie

Table of Contents

Part I   Uncertain Times

Part II   On the Way

Part   Letting Go

Part IV   Seven Years Later

Part I

Uncertain Times

Chapter I
At Home

War News: World War II
1917 – 1938

When World War I ended, the world was in turmoil. The Russian revolutions, begun in 1917, were still continuing. The Versailles Treaty had left Germany with impossible war reparations. In Italy, Benito Mussolini was leading his country into fascism. Civil War between the Nationalists and the Communists had erupted in China. Japan, seeking to become a world power, had invaded Manchuria and many of the small islands in the Pacific. In Spain, the Fascists were fighting the Socialists. But the rise of the Nazi State with Adolf Hitler in power in Germany seemed the most disturbing to the residents in Hoskins, Nebraska and to the surrounding farming community.

*   *   *

As Europe was entering desperate times, Walter and Lisetta Getzmer were struggling with the Great Depression in the United States. For two years they had experienced severe hardship on the farm they were renting from Minnie Meritz, Lisetta's mother. First, a drought destroyed most of their corn; then a torrential rain beat down any remaining stalks. The next year they again experienced drought, followed by sleeping sickness for one of their horses, and the devastation of a grasshopper invasion.

To prepare for the winter ahead, they butchered a steer and a pig and prepared smoked sausages and had canned chunks of beef and pork. With their two small children, Jeannine and Fauneil, they moved into a small rental house in Hoskins, the nearest village to Minnie's farm.

Shortly after being situated, Frank Contras, his wife Mabel, and their two boys came from Chicago to Hoskins to find work with the Works Progress Administration (WPA), about which Walter had written them. The WPA had just begun building a road from Hoskins to Winside. When the two men applied for jobs, Walter was hired to move dirt with a team of horses for 75 cents a day, and Frank was offered a dollar a day to be the timekeeper.

To celebrate the men's good fortune, Walter and Lisetta had invited the Contras family for Sunday-noon dinner. For the occasion, Lisetta opened a jar of her delicious canned beef. She used the juice in the jar to make gravy for the mashed potatoes. Home-canned corn, green beans, homemade bread, and peach pie completed the meal. Following dinner, the children went outside to play while the adults remained around the table to visit.

"I can't believe these times," said Mabel. "There was an article in the paper with the headline **Debtless Nebraska Has $4.27 in the Treasury**. Imagine only $4.27 in the treasury."

"At least the state is debtless," said Walter. "That's more than you can say for the federal government."

"Ja, the New Deal is expensive," added Frank, "and it doesn't seem to be working. The depression is as bad today as it was five years ago."

"Maybe worse, "said Lisetta, "and President Roosevelt isn't handling international issues well."

Mabel agreed. "He didn't support the League of Nations' effort to stabilize currency, so the U.S. isn't the only country in this depression."

"Aggressors like Hitler are using the depression to stir up the Germans," added Walter, "and not just Hitler, but Mussolini in Italy; and Japan has been moving against Manchuria. We're getting closer to war. Hitler" --

"Ja," Mabel interrupted her brother. "There's been a lot about Hitler on the radio. He's built the German military up to over a million men. No peaceful nation needs that many men trained for war."

Walter nodded. "We still have relatives in Germany – Uncle Richard's family. I wonder what they think of Hitler."

*   *   *

At the end of the week, Walter and Frank received their first paychecks at the WPA, but Walter received a layoff notice as well.

"What's the meaning of this?" he asked the clerk.

"I don't know. I just pass 'em out. See the manager on Monday." All weekend long, Walter wondered what he could possibly have done wrong. On Monday he found out. An employee in the administration had seen him drive to work in his 1937 Ford and felt that Walter's job should be given to someone who really needed it. When Walter told Lisetta the reason for the layoff, she asked him, "Why didn't you explain our financial situation?"

"I did say that I had a wife and two girls to support, but I couldn't tell them about my summer work adjusting hail losses. They want someone who can work year 'round, or until they no longer need him. So, until summertime, we don't even have my seventy-five-cents-a-day income."

Lisetta had an idea. "Why don't we pay a visit to Herb and Irene Mittlestadt this evening? Herb has a government job and may know of one coming up." The visit brought hope. Herb knew that the job of postmistress or postmaster was open for applicants who would take a civil service examination.

"I don't want it," explained Herb. "I'm happy working outdoors as a mail carrier. Why don't you stop by the post office tomorrow, Walt, and pick up an application and the exam information?"

Walter filled out the application, took the exam, and waited for the results. January and February brought no news. Walter and Lisetta scrimped even more. Walter still had his small insurance income from the business Mr. Rohrke had sold him when Walter had worked at the Hoskins Bank. This paid the rent and the utilities, but there was no money for gas, clothes, or food. Fortunately, Irene Mittlestadt gave Lisetta her daughter's old clothing, which Lisetta ripped apart to sew outfits for the girls. Minnie helped by bringing in from the farm eggs, chickens, fruit and vegetables. Walt's dad provided milk and cream from the acreage.

"It would be nice to spend a quarter for some gas," complained Walter to Lisetta.

"Be patient, Walt. You'll know about that job soon. Keep your spirits up! Keep busy. Help your dad on the acreage or your brother Emil on his farm. Remember how much Emil helped us when we were on the farm. This is your chance to repay him."

In March, Walter and Lisetta had a visitor. Helen Cross, the secretary-treasurer for the credit association (the co-op), came to tell Walter in person that she had gotten the job as postmistress. When Walter's face fell, she said, "I'll be leaving my job at the co-op, and I was thinking that with your experience in the Hoskins Bank, you would make a fine replacement for me. You already know the members of the co-op. They were customers at the Hoskins Bank before it closed."

Walter's face lit up. "What's the pay?"

"Thirty dollars a month."

"Wow! That's a fortune!

Helen laughed. "I'll put in a good word for you when I speak to the board."

Weeks later, Walter stepped into the co-op to say hello to Helen Cross and to ask about the status of a job for him. Henry Kruger, a member of the co-op, came in to make a payment on his farm loan. Walter asked him how it was going, and Henry complained about not being able to sell his crops.

"I can't sell them for peanuts, Walt. I'm ready to give it all up. Want to buy my farm? Only $8,000 for 160 acres."

"I don't have one thousand, let alone eight."

"You don't need eight. Take over my farm loan with Prudential for $5,500 and that leaves only $2,500 down payment."

"Henry, you'd better look elsewhere for a buyer. I can barely provide for my family."

The seed had been planted. After Henry had left, Walter did some calculating. If he got the job at the co-op for thirty a month, plus his hail adjuster's income from May to September, he might be able to do it. That evening, he told Lisetta about August's proposal and asked, "Is it a pipe dream?"

"No. Before we were married, you told me about your dream to own land. I'm willing to help you to achieve that. I could take over at the co-op when you're 'on the road,' but I would need someone to look after the girls."

"It would take years to raise cash for the down payment. We're already scrimping and saving in a house with no plumbing."

"This depression can't last forever, Walt."

Chapter II
Life and Death

War News
1939 – 1940

On March 15, 1939, Germany marched into Czechoslovakia, making it a vassal state of Germany. England and France recruited soldiers for their armies, threatening to respond if Poland was invaded. On September 1, 1939, Germany invaded Poland, and on September 3rd, Britain and France declared war on Germany.

Because of the strength and efficacy of the German Panzer divisions and their air force, the Luftwaffe, Germany moved quickly to invade Denmark and Norway, followed by the "Blitzkrieg" (the invasion of Luxembourg, Belgium, the Netherlands, and France.) The British Expeditionary Force (BEF), composed of two-thirds British and one-third French, was in danger of being destroyed at Dunkirk, a seaport in northern France, where the Germans had them trapped. From May 27th through June 3rd, 340,000 of the BEF were rescued by the British Navy and a flotilla of ferry boats and small British civilian crafts, in spite of being heavily strafed by the Luftwaffe. It was a combination of military and civilian heroism and ingenuity.

*　　*　　*

Walter and Lisetta were waiting for guests. Lisetta warned Jeannine and Fauneil: "You girls had better behave yourselves today. We have guests coming for dinner."

"Who's comin'?"

"Grandma Meritz and your father's brother Hank, his wife Tillie, and their three boys. They're stopping here on their way from Chicago to California. Now wash up and put on those dresses I laid out for you."

When Hank arrived, he hugged Walter and Lisetta, shook hands with Minnie, and introduced his wife and their three boys.

"The last time I saw you, Zettie, you were a little girl with a braid hanging down your back. You were crying because you didn't want me to go, and I promised you that I would see you again. And here I am."

"It took an awfully long time to keep your promise, Hank," responded Lisetta.

"I know. I've been gone so long, I hardly recognized Hoskins. I've been telling Tillie all about the Hoskins I knew, but it's not here anymore. Hoskins is like a ghost town."

"Ghost is the wrong word," responded Walter. "Spirit, maybe – yes, a spirit town. The community still has quite a few old-timers whose parents pioneered this area."

Hank addressed Minnie. "I was sorry to hear about your husband, Gus."

"That was twelve years ago that he died. My son Lyle and his family live in that big house now, and I built a smaller one across the road where you used to 'batch' for yourself."

"I have good memories of those days – you bringing me *Kaffeekuchen*, Zettie, and sitting down on the prairie grass to eat it; my dad and your dad getting tipsy on homemade elderberry wine; and Gus coming over the hill, half-asleep, with the horses in charge. When they turned down the lane, they were excited and galloped fast, heading for the barn."

Hank looked at Minnie. "You were waiting, hands on hips, on the porch and yelled at Gus when he didn't rein them back. I thought they were going to run right into the barn door, but at the last minute, they abruptly stopped, and Gus almost fell off the spring wagon."

Everyone laughed except Minnie, who shook her head. "That was Gus! He and your dad were good friends, but sometimes they were a bad influence on each other."

As Hank and his family were leaving, Hank took Walter aside and said softly, "Do you think you'll be called up if the U.S. gets involved in this war?"

"I don't know, Hank. More and more countries are getting caught up in it. I remember that I was still in school when you were called up for World War I, and the Germans surrendered unconditionally just as you got to Chicago."

"And here we go again with Germany. Stay safe, Walt!"

* * *

By spring, Walter was working at the co-op. His former position at the bank and his new one opened up other business opportunities as well. His insurance business began to expand; he was able to sell wind, rain, and hail policies to farmers who sought his advice. Two of his clients, Bertha and Hertha Beilenberg, were so pleased with his advice, they asked him to take over the management of their farms.

Bertha and Hertha were as different as towels and trowels. Bertha loved the indoors. She did the cooking, baking, cleaning, laundering, and sewing. Hertha loved the outdoors. She cared for the outside of the house and her garden, which she strove to make the prettiest in town. If she spotted in the neighborhood a bearded iris more magnificent than any of hers, she plucked it off at the top of the stem and stuffed it into her pocket, leaving the stem bare.

Unlike Hertha, Bertha liked people. When Walter came to see them, sometimes accompanied by Jeannine and Fauneil, Bertha gave the girls cookies or pieces of cake. Hertha was aloof. She sat on the bench of the roller piano, half-turned away from her company. If a question needed her answer as well as Bertha's, she responded in curt, haltering phrases.

When hail adjusting season began, Walter hired Bertha as housekeeper and caregiver. Because Bertha was not a disciplinarian, Jeannine and Fauneil spent most of their summer days outside unsupervised. They walked to Grandma and Grandpa Getzmer's acreage, where they climbed on top of the hen house and watched the chickens scratching below. Next, they climbed a large maple tree in the front yard, which gave them a good view of the road. When they tired of sitting in the tree, they pushed each other on the porch swing. Sometimes their grandma heard the squeaking of the swing and brought out some cookies to eat. As they were leaving the acreage, they picked Concord grapes growing along the fence.

In town they wandered in and out of buildings: the grocery store, the lumber store, the post office, but not the co-op. Lisetta did not want them "traipsing" about town.

"Why don't we try to get into the old hotel? There is a door at the top of those steps," said Jeannine. She led the way up the steps. "Be careful," she said, indicating a wasp's nest, but she was too late. As Fauneil stepped into the nest, the angry wasps stung her on her feet, legs, and thighs. To stop Fauneil's wailing, Jeannine took her by the hand and led her down the steps and then headed for the schoolyard, which had an outdoor pump.

"Mud is good for stings," she explained as she turned on the faucet and made mud from the dirt and the water. Meanwhile, Lisetta had closed up the co-op, had purchased two bags of groceries, and was heading home past the Mittlestadt house. Irene was on the porch swing reading the newspaper. She motioned for Lisetta to join her.

"What's in the news?" Lisetta asked.

"The war in Europe. The Germans are using U-boats to sink British ships, and the U.S. is allowing delivery of war supplies to Britain and France. It won't be long before one of our ships is sunk by a U-boat."

"You're right. We're not staying neutral." Irene pointed. "Say, Lisetta, aren't those your two little girls across the street?"

"You bet, and they've been traipsing around town again. I'd better get home!" She got home before the girls had had time to clean up, and a scolding and a spanking followed. Alone in their bedroom, the girls discussed it.

"We'd better be careful when Dad is gone."

"Ja, Mom is crabbier then.

*   *   *

War News
1940

The war widened from Western Europe to engulf countries in Africa, the Mideast and the East. The Allies and the Axis were evolving into the major powers.

*On June 10th, Italy declared war on France and Britain.
*On August 3rd, Italian forces entered British Somaliland in East Africa.
*On September 27th, Germany, Italy, and Japan signed the Tripartite Pact, becoming the Axis.
*On October 18th, Britain opened the Burma Road, which was a vital supply route to Chinese forces fighting the Japanese.
*On November 20th, Hungary joined the Tripartite Pact.
*On November 23rd, Romania joined the Tripartite Pact.
*In December, Greek forces pushed Italian forces back of the Albanian border, stopping an invasion.

*   *   *

On Sunday, September 19, 1939, Wilhem and Emelia Getzmer celebrated their 50th anniversary. In the afternoon, there was an open house at the Getzmer acreage. More than 200 people were in and out of the dining room for refreshments. Wilhelm had made many friends in the areas of Winside and Hoskins, where they had farmed.

It was a day for reminiscing. Emelia stood by while Wilhelm talked about their roots in West Prussia; their emigration to America in 1893; their life in Cleveland before moving to Winside; the purchase of their farm near Hoskins; the death of three children and the raising of seven boys and two girls;

and the selling of their farm to their son Emil and moving to the acreage.

The Bruce Pavilion had been rented for the evening, and a local band had been hired for an anniversary dance. The evening opened with a waltz for Wilhelm and Emelia. It was the only time Emelia danced all evening because of her crippled feet. However, Wilhelm spent the rest of the evening dancing the schottische and the polka with his older granddaughters.

The next day, the couple resumed their daily routines. Emelia milked the cows, ran and cleaned the separator, and did her household chores. Wilhelm worked in the garden and delivered milk and cream to his regular customers in Hoskins. As usual, the last house on his route was Walter's and Lisetta's. When he arrived, Jeannine and Fauneil were outside playing in the yard.

"Girls," he asked, "vould you like to go to zeh store *mit* Grandpa?" The girls ran to the cart. "Here, take ziss *Milch* to your mama und tell her."

When they returned, he lifted them onto the cart and pulled them to the grocery store. Wilhelm sold his milk and cream and then gave each of them a penny to spend. Jeannine chose several sticks of black licorice, and Fauneil selected a sucker. On the way back home, he sang to them in German as he pulled them on the cart.

When Walter got home from work, Lisetta said to him, "Walt, I don't think your dad should be pulling that heavy cart anymore. Today when he brought the girls back from the grocery store, his face was beet red, and he was puffing."

"Zettie, he loves to give the girls a ride. He isn't as strong as he was, but he still has the spirit to make them happy. They'll remember it, even though they're only four and five."

At four o'clock in the morning, Walter and Lisetta were awakened by someone knocking on the door. Walter got up, put on his robe and slippers, and answered the door. It was Pastor Bittorf.

"I just came from your parents' home. Your father has passed away, Walter."

"His heart?"

"Yes. Evidently, he started having pains and difficulty breathing about two o'clock this morning. He knew he was dying. He was frightened and sent your mother to get me. She walked to our house in the dark to ask me to come. When I got there, he was still conscious. I heard his confession, administered absolution, and prayed for him. He slipped into a coma and died a short while later."

Lisetta, who had joined them in the living room said, "I'm glad he was at peace with God. Emelia will want him to have a Christian burial."

"I need to talk with the elders of the church about that. You know the church doesn't allow unbelievers a Christian burial."

"Dad was a believer!" shouted Walter. "He left the church after my baby brother died such a painful death. Dad didn't understand how a good God could allow a little tyke to suffer such misery."

"Well, you know, none of us can look into another man's heart. Your dad did ask for and did receive absolution. I think I can convince the elders to let God be the judge."

Three days later, the funeral took place in the Trinity Evangelical Lutheran Church in Hoskins. It was almost as well-attended as Gus Meritz's funeral had been twelve years prior. Like his best friend, Gus, Wilhelm had been well-liked and respected.

Following the service, the long funeral procession left Hoskins and headed east towards the Pleasant View Cemetery outside of Winside. On the way, Lisetta sat thinking about her father's funeral procession to Norfolk. She rolled down the window to inhale the sweet smell of the prairie vegetation, as she had done that day. When they neared Winside, she saw the road across from the cemetery, leading over a little stream and running past the picturesque town, with its houses staggering up the hillside.

"You know, Zettie, my father was the center of attention at Fleer's Store when he brought his farm products into town to sell. There were chairs located on the wooden sidewalk outside the store. After he finished selling, he always took a seat outside to smoke a cigar. Other farmers gathered around to be entertained by his jokes and stories. Remember that picture we have of him in his overalls and straw hat, holding a cigar in his hand?"

Lisetta nodded. Following the graveside ceremony, the family returned to the acreage for refreshments and visiting.

Ruby Getzmer, Bill's wife, came up to Lisetta in the dining room, put her arm around her waist, and asked, "When is your baby due, Zettie?"

"In September. We're hoping for a boy this time."

"Funny how that goes in families. We've had four boys, and you seem to be inclined to have girls." Just then Fauneil joined them with a piece of cake in her hand.

"What do you have there?" asked Ruby.

"C-c-c-cake," answered Fauneil and ran off to play with her cousin, Donna.

"I didn't know Fauneil stuttered," commented Ruby.

"She's just started it. She's had a hard time lately. She lost her best companion when Jeannine started school. Then she was scared by a bull snake. She knocked out her four front teeth when she fell in an accident with her little red wagon. Now her grandpa is dead, and soon she won't be the baby of the family any longer."

"Little ones have their problems, too," responded Ruby.

Lisetta saw Minnie visiting with Emelia and walked over to join them. "Well, Ma," she said, "I'll bet Dad is happy. Now he has his best friend with him to play *Schafskopf* again."

"Ja," agreed Minnie. She turned to Emelia. "You lost a husband, Emelia, and my Gus gained a friend. *The Lord giveth and the Lord taketh away.* Emelia nodded in silence.

* * *

Chapter III
Closer to War

War News
1940 – 1941

Hitler attempted to invade Britain across the channel by Operation Sealion, but the British navy was a formidable deterrent. Hitler soon transferred his intentions to destroying the Royal Air Force (RAF) in the Battle of Britain, a nine-month bombing campaign against London and other industrial cities. The RAF lost so many planes and aviators, that they were at the point of defeat when Hitler suddenly turned his attention to the invasion of Russia.

*　　*　　*

Walter sat reading the war news. As Lisetta entered the room, he looked up and said, "The war news isn't good, but at least the British are not defeated."

"Is it affecting us badly, Walt, here in the middle of the U.S?"

"Well, yes, in a sense. Henry Kruger is after me again to buy his farm, but if the U.S. gets into the war, I might be drafted. And then you'd have the responsibilities of a farm, our home, our girls, and the co-op."

"I know it."

"Henry keeps putting on the pressure. He wants a sale now, and we're still five hundred dollars short."

"Why don't you go into Norfolk and try for a loan at the bank?"

"We don't have any collateral for a loan. They'd just laugh at me."

"No one has any collateral now, and there are farms waiting to be purchased. Just smile, Walt, and be your charming self."

Walter drove into Norfolk and met with Mr. DeLay of the DeLay National Bank. Walter introduced himself, described his background, the history of his work, and his ambition to own a farm. Then he handed Mr. DeLay a piece of paper on which he had typed the pertinent information:

Wayne County XX Quarter, Section XX.   Price $8,000
Loan from Prudential Insurance   5,500
Cash on hand   2,000
Cash needed for down payment   500

"You've managed to save $2,000 during this depression?" asked Mr. DeLay.

"My wife and I have, but we don't have collateral for the $500."

"I'm impressed," said Mr. DeLay. "As for the $500, your face is good enough for me. You have your loan."

Lisetta was right, Walter thought as he drove home. *A smile and a confident spirit can help a dream come true. Just stay positive now*, he advised himself.

*   *   *

In late September of 1940, Lisetta was due to give birth to her third child. Marcella, her brother Lyle's wife, had delivered her third child in June. As the time neared for Lisetta, Walter drove Jeannine and Fauneil to Minnie's farm for a brief stay. While the girls were there, Minnie walked them across the road to see their baby cousin, Lane.

"He's so tiny!" exclaimed Jeannine.

"And cute!" added Fauneil.

"Ja," answered Minnie. "Your baby will be tiny and cute, too."

When Minnie brought the girls home, Lisetta took them to the bassinet to see the newborn.

"This is your baby sister, Marleen. Isn't she beautiful?"

The girls didn't answer. All they could see was a red face and puffy eyes.

"It's too bad that Walt's father didn't get to see the baby," said Lisetta to Minnie.

"Or your own father, Zettie."

"That's right, Ma. That's right."

* * *

The baptismal dinner for Marleen was held at the acreage, with the Getzmer relatives and Minnie attending.

"How are you getting along, Emelia?" asked Minnie. "Are you able to keep up with the milking and the chickens and the house and the garden?"

Mabel answered for her mother. "Frank and I are helping out at the acreage. I don't think Mother could keep it up on her own." Emelia shook her head in disagreement, but said nothing.

Minnie addressed Frank. "Lisetta tells me you're moving to California."

"Yes, there's a lot of work out there in the defense industry now that Britain is buying tanks from the U.S."

"So, Walt, will you be looking after Emelia when Mabel and Frank move to California?"

Walter and Mabel exchanged a look, an indication that they had already spoken about this matter. Walter addressed his mother. "Those basement steps are too steep for you, Mother. We all worry about your falling and hurting yourself."

"I'm careful, Valter. I von't fall. Ziss is my home."

Soft-spoken, retiring Emelia was no match for her children. As soon as the Contras family moved to California, Emelia was taken to live with her daughter, Annie. The plan was for each of her children to take turns caring for her. The acreage was rented by Walter and Lisetta. In lieu of paying Emelia rent for the first few months, Walter made improvements to the property: the walk-in pantry was transformed into a bathroom with plumbing (now the family would have the luxury of an indoor toilet instead of a wooden outhouse), the hand pump at the kitchen sink was replaced with hot and cold-water faucets, and new linoleum was laid on the kitchen floor.

*   *   *

War News
1940 – 1941

In July 1940, Prime Minister Winston Churchill sought help from the U.S. He appealed to President Roosevelt for 50 old destroyers. Roosevelt agreed, but in return, he wanted 99-year leases on sea and airbases in the British West Indies and Bermuda. When the Lend-Lease Act was finally passed by Congress, it allowed Britain to borrow war supplies from the U.S. for later repayment. In 1940, the U.S. produced 346 tanks; by 1944, the defense industry had produced 17,500.

*   *   *

During the summer of 1941, Walter was on the road, adjusting crop losses, earning and saving money in an effort to pay off his farm loans as quickly as possible. Lisetta took his place at the co-op, and Bertha Beilenberg again worked as their housekeeper and baby-sitter. Bertha doted on baby Marleen, leaving Jeannine and Fauneil to take care of themselves.

One summer afternoon, Lisetta arrived home tired. She was carrying two sacks of groceries, which she had purchased after work. As she approached the back porch at the acreage, she stepped into a hole filled with water, pitched forward, and almost fell and dropped her bags of groceries.

"Jeannine! Fauneil!" she called angrily. The girls came sheepishly out of the barn. "I've told you before," she reprimanded, "No digging! I just stepped into this big hole here and almost fell. These holes are dangerous! If I catch you digging again, you'll get a spanking." Jeannine and Fauneil were quiet, afraid to risk saying the wrong thing. They knew what a spanking meant. Mom would go to a willow tree, tear off a green switch, strip it of its leaves, and swish it back and forth. The sight and sound of the willow switch would be almost as bad as the stings on the buttocks and thighs.

*   *   *

When school started in the fall, the girls had less time for naughty behavior. Jeannine entered the third grade and Fauneil the second. Their teacher, Miss Zimmerman, taught all eight grades in the same classroom at the parochial school. Just as Lisetta had organized her school day when she had taught rural school, Miss Zimmerman arranged recitation time following study time throughout the day. Because Fauneil was the only student in her grade, she received less individual attention from Miss Zimmerman. Consequently, Fauneil learned primarily by listening to the lessons of the older students.

With Walter through with adjusting hail losses for the season, the family sat down together for the evening meal. On December 7th, Walter and Lisetta visited for a while before Walter turned on the radio to Station WJAG in Norfolk, just in time for an announcement:

"An attack on Pearl Harbor in Hawaii started at 7:55 a.m., local time in Hawaii. The bombing severely crippled our Pacific Naval Fleet. Within an hour, five of our eight battleships were sinking, and the Arizona was completely destroyed. President Roosevelt has called *Dec. 7, 1941 a date that will live in infamy.*"

"Gosh!" gasped Lisetta. Walter responded in a hushed, emotional tone. "I knew it would not be long before our soldiers would be fighting in the Pacific and, no doubt, in Europe. Now it's here."

As soon as Minnie learned about Pearl Harbor, she called Lisetta on the telephone.

"Is Walt worried about the war?"

"Ja, he's only thirty-five, young enough to get drafted."

"Well, they'll draft the young single men first, like they did in the last war."

"That should save Walt and Lyle for the time being."

"I don't think Lyle will have to go," said Minnie. "They like to keep the farmers on the land. The troops will need food, you know."

"Ma, Walt has a farm, too, almost paid for."

"But you don't actually live on the land, Zettie. The government wouldn't consider him a farmer."

The next day, Minnie called again. "Zettie, the Bech mausoleum was struck by lightning in yesterday's storm. I'm told that it's been destroyed. Go out and have a look at it and then call me back."
When Walter came home from the co-op, he and Lisetta drove out to the cemetery. As they approached the gravesite, they could see that the mausoleum no longer dominated the

cemetery. Where a tall red-brick structure had stood on an elevated white-tile foundation, there were now two lone caskets, those of Lisetta's grandparents. Lisetta looked around at the poorly kept graves, the groves of dark trees at the top of the hill, and the lonely stream meandering at the bottom. She shivered.

"This is a desolate place. I don't know what Ma will do with these caskets, but I'm sure she won't build another mausoleum here."

"Didn't you tell me once that your grandfather, August Bech, wanted this mausoleum built as his final resting place?"

"Ja," Lisetta answered. "He was such a proud, foolish man. He'll have to take a humble place in the earth now, like the rest of these people."

Walter turned his attention to the humble graves around him. Two had been soldiers: Cyril Templin, a Civil War Veteran, 1837 – 1935 and Ernest Bech, who dies in World War I, 1894 – 1918.
"Wasn't Ernest Bech a relative of your grandfather, Lisetta?"

"Ja, Ernest Bech was his stepson. Ernest's father died the first winter my grandmother homesteaded on the prairie. The following spring, Augusta married August, and they must have changed Ernest's name to Bech when he was about four years old."

"Ernest was younger when he died than I am now," remarked Walter. "I hope Pearl Harbor and this lightning strike aren't a bad omen."

"For you, Walt?"

"For us, Lisetta. I'm sure to be called up."

"The single men will be taken first. Don't dwell on what might happen, Walt."

"This is the place we'll all end up, Lisetta, wartime or peacetime."

"But not now. Not yet." Lisetta turned away and looked across to a pasture where cattle were grazing, aware only of their momentary contentment.

*   *   *

War News
1941 – 1942

By 1941, the war in Europe had spread to Africa, Libya, Greece, Iraq, Syria, and Lebanon. When Germany invaded Russia, Romania and Italy declared war on Russia. In the Pacific, Japan joined the Axis powers. After the bombing of Pearl Harbor, the U.S. and Britain declared war on Japan. Now the U.S. would be fighting in two arenas: Europe, under the leadership of General Dwight D. Eisenhower and the Pacific, under the command of General Douglas MacArthur.

*   *   *

The summer of 1942 was a difficult time for Walter and Lisetta. They were worried that Walter would be called up. If that happened, they would be separated, and Lisetta would have to cope alone. Walter was concerned that he might lose his farm as well as his life. Working more was his way of dealing with his worry. He decided to take on additional responsibility with the Omaha Rain and Hail Bureau. His manager, Art Post, offered him the job of team supervisor. In addition to Walter's regular work in the fields, he would be responsible for mapping out assignments and for studying all of the claims which the other adjustors submitted for farmers, making sure that they were reasonable and accurate.

Walter informed Lisetta. "It will add hours to my workday, but it will mean more money."

"You're already overworked, Walt, and I'll bet you have an ulcer from eating at those *greasy spoons*."

Lisetta's workday was increased, as well, with family responsibilities and managing the co-op. Her solution to the work load was to have Bertha take care of Marleen again, and from time to time, to send Jeannine and Fauneil to stay with Minnie at her farm.

Minnie was happy to have them with her. She put them to work, lessening her own tasks, while teaching them about farm life. She showed them how to pick strawberries – separating the vines from the hidden berries, picking each berry close to the vine, and then pinching off the runners so that the vines would produce more berries.

She demonstrated to them how to milk: squeezing and pulling one teat with one hand and simultaneously a second teat with the other. After the cows had been milked, the girls learned how to run the separator to separate the milk from the cream, and how to wash the separator afterwards to keep it clean.

Helping Minnie prepare fried chicken was their least favorite task. Minnie did the first steps alone: catching a rooster, holding it by its legs over an old tree stump, and chopping its head off with a hatchet. The girls watched as the headless rooster hopped around a bit before plopping down dead. After Minnie had soaked the rooster in hot water, the girls' job was to pluck the feathers off the bird and then singe the pin feathers. Before frying the chicken, Minnie cut the chicken open and showed them how to pull out the innards: the liver, heart, kidneys, intestines, and gizzard. The intestines were given to the pigs to eat, and the other innards were steamed in hot water to add to the gravy. The chicken was then cut into pieces, which were floured and seasoned with salt and pepper. At last, the chicken was ready for frying.

The reward for the day was a meal of fried chicken, mashed potatoes and gravy, vegetables, and fresh strawberries. In the evening, Minnie, Jeannine, and Fauneil were ready for a rest. Minnie sat in a rocking chair on her screened-in porch and embroidered while she told them stories about her past. Fauneil was especially intrigued.

"You should write those down, Grandma," she suggested, "so people could read about them."

"I don't write well, Fauneil," answered Minnie. "You write them down."

*   *   *

War News
1942

Japan became an increasing threat in the Pacific in 1942.

*On January 2nd, Japanese forces captured Manila in the Philippines.
*On February 8th Japan, having already secured a base in Siam, invaded Burma.
*On May 5th, Japanese forces landed on the island of Corregidor.
*On May 6th, the Allies surrendered Corregidor to Japan.
*From June 4th – 7th, after heavy fighting, Japan was defeated on the Island of Midway. It lost four of its carriers.

On September 15th, the U.S. lost a carrier when a Japanese submarine torpedoed it.

Japan was well on its way to becoming a world power.

*   *   *

When school started in the fall of 1942, Jeannine and Fauneil found that Miss Zimmerman had resigned, and Miss Gruber had taken her place. Whereas Miss Zimmerman had been experienced, organized, and strict with her pupils, Miss Gruber was new to teaching and couldn't handle the students well in the classroom or outside at recess time.

In the fall of the year, the kids played baseball, and supervision was not needed. But when winter brought cold, snow, and ice, the children needed supervision. Miss Gruber expected the older ones to take care of the younger ones while she remained inside, preparing for the next lesson.

On a cold, icy day in March, the boys and girls were engaged in a skating contest. The boys had made a long strip of ice by stomping down fresh snow and slush, letting it freeze overnight, and smoothing it into an ice strip the next day. The pupils lined up on opposite sides of the strip, boys on one side, girls on the other. Each individual had to take a long run, hop onto the ice, balance a slide, and hop off into a snowbank. Boys and girls alternated turns; whichever side had fewer falls won the game.

When Fauneil's turn came, she took a long run and hopped onto the ice. When each foot was down, with one leg forward, one back, she used her arms to balance her body, like a bird in flight. It was a thrilling experience! Suddenly, Dwight, an older boy, reached out and pushed her from behind. Unable to keep her balance, and with no time to protect herself, Fauneil smashed into the ice, with her left eye and bone above it taking the full force of the blow. For a second, she heard the crack of the bone, and then experienced blackness.

Jeannine ran into the school to tell Miss Gruber, who sent her to run home to fetch her mother. When Lisetta came with the car, she had towels to wrap around Fauneil's head. She told Jeannine to ride in the backseat of the car and to hold her sister's head in her lap. In spite of the snowy roads, Lisetta sped for Norfolk to Dr. Brauer's office at lightning speed. After examining Fauneil, he stitched her wounds and bandaged her. He advised Lisetta: "Keep her at home while she heals; remove the bandages each morning; use hot compresses to open the eye; clean away the draining pus; apply ointment; and rebandage the area."

Although Lisetta followed Dr. Brauer's orders, Fauneil's eye oozed pus for several months. Lisetta kept Fauneil home until the end of the school year. The eye and bone finally healed, but the bone remained puffy for most of Fauneil's school years.

During Fauneil's convalescence, Walter received a notice from the draft board, ordering him to report to Winside.

"It's finally come, Lisetta. I hope they find something wrong with me."

"I hope they don't. I hope you **stress** that you have a wife and three girls at home who need you."

Walter drove to Winside the next day, had a physical exam by a doctor, and visited with a sergeant he knew from his WPA days. He was told that he would be rated for fitness and should go home and wait for the results. Several days later, Lisetta called him on the telephone at the co-op.

"Good news! You don't have to go. You were rated 4-F"

"4-F! I surely must be better fit than that!"

"Be grateful, Walt. It's only because of your flat feet."

"Flat feet!" Walter laughed. "Saved by my flat feet. All that walking in the cornfields. Good old fallen arches." He reflected a moment. "Thank God that worry is over."

*   *   *

War News
1943

The Allies turned the tide of the European war in their favor.

*On January 27th, the U.S. launched its first air raid on the German cities of Emden and Wilhelmshaven.
*On January 31st, Hitler's Sixth Army surrendered to Russia at Stalingrad after doing extensive damage to the city.
*Rommel forced an Allied withdrawal in Tunisia.
*On May 13th, the Allies rallied to capture 240,000 Axis soldiers, forcing a surrender of Italy's First Army.
*On July 10th, the Allies landed in Sicily with over 2,500 ships in an amphibious assault.

From July 24th – August 3rd, Hamburg was the target of massive bombing raids.

On August 17th, the Americans entered Messina, Italy.

On September 11th, German forces took control of the major Italian cities of Rome, Milan, Bologna, and Verona.

A month later, when Italy declared war on Germany; the Axis lost one of their major partners.

*   *   *

Chapter V
Better Days

In the fall of 1943 when school resumed, Lisetta sent the girls to the Hoskins Public School instead of the parochial school. They wouldn't get any religious instruction there, but the teacher, Mrs. Fuhrman, was experienced and well-organized. Jeannine and Fauneil fell in love with her bubbling personality. During supervised recess time, they became better acquainted with their cousins, Donna and Paul, who attended the school and lived next door to it.

Walter, who was now the chairman of the board of trustees for the co-op, came home at nine o'clock one evening from a meeting of the board.

"That was an important meeting, Lisetta. The co-op has grown so much that we agreed we should try to become a state bank – like we were before the depression."

"Well, why not just stay a co-op?"

"A state bank can transact certain types of business that a credit association can't. If we want to continue to grow, we need to expand our range of transactions."

In order to achieve bank status, Walter needed to go to the Capitol Building in Lincoln to apply for a charter. Leaving the next day, he drove through Wisner, Beemer, West Point, Scribner, Hooper, Fremont, and Wahoo, arriving too late to go to the Capitol.

After checking in at a hotel near the Capitol, he strolled along "O" Street. Servicemen were going in and out of a

34

canteen. Walter stopped in to see what a canteen was like. Along one wall was a long refreshment table, where women were serving the soldiers. A band was playing, and couples were two-stepping and jitterbugging. Walter stood awhile watching and listening as the band played "Don't Sit under the Apple Tree." A young woman approached Walter and asked him to dance. He declined and headed for the door as the vocalist in the band began singing,

"Mareseatoatsanddoeseatoatsandlittlelambseativy"

"Akid'lleativytoo. Wouldn't you?" sang a soldier, extending his hand to the young woman.

As Walter headed back to the hotel, he was thinking: H*ow young the soldiers are, how full of spirit, how optimistic and carefree! In a short time, they'll be overseas on a battlefront, in a hospital, or lying dead.* He said a brief prayer for their safety and one of thanks that he had been spared serving.

* * *

War News
1943

In the Pacific, the fighting was a combined effort by navy, marines, and air force.

*From February 1ˢᵗ – 7ᵗʰ, the Battle for Guadalcanal ended with the Japanese evacuating.
*From March 2ⁿᵈ – 4ᵗʰ, U.S. B-25s sank 12 Japanese ships bound for New Guinea.
*From April 7ᵗʰ – 18ᵗʰ, the Japanese air offensive over the Solomon Islands and eastern New Guinea was defeated.

Admiral Yamamoto, who planned the attack on Pearl Harbor, was killed when U.S. fighters shot down his plane.
U.S. forces landed in the Gilbert Islands.
Combined Australian and U.S. troops landed at Nassau Bay near Salamaua, New Guinea.

The Allies were succeeding in capturing tiny island bases held by Japan, but the cost of American lives was high. The Japanese soldiers' defense was fearless, at times even "fanatical."

* * *

Before Walter left Lincoln, he toured the capitol building, joining a group led by a young female guide. She relayed the history of the building to them:

"Groundbreaking began in 1922. The new building was built without tearing the old one down. The large square base was built first, around the old building. Then they tore down the old building and erected the tower in the center. The base represents the flat plains of Nebraska, and the tower symbolizes the dreams of the pioneers.

"The huge pink marble columns supporting the high ceiling in the foyer were imported from Italy. They were shipped across the ocean and delivered by train. The engineers built a railroad siding around the structure and tore out the tracks after the marble columns were in place and the building was finished. In the tower section, the walls shoot up over 300 feet to the dome of the rotunda. The mosaics on the floors symbolize the Spirits of Nebraska: the Spirit of the Soil, the Spirit of Vegetation, and the Spirit of Animal Life. The mosaics on the ceiling depict the Gifts of Nature to Man on the Plains: plowing, sowing, cultivating, and reaping.

"When you leave the Capitol," said the guide, "be sure to look up at the top of the dome where you'll see the statue of The Sower, which is 19 feet tall. The Sower has a huge bag of seeds slung over his left shoulder; his left hand is holding the bag open; his right arm is back in a throwing position; and his hand is cupped as if sowing seeds."

That's the perfect symbol for Nebraska, Walter thought, as he looked up at The Sower from the sidewalk.

When he arrived home, he described the capitol building to Lisetta and promised to take her there sometime.

"Good! Do that sometime. Did you get what you needed?"

"Yes. I got the information for the charter and picked up all of the forms I need to fill out. By the end of March, the co-op will be the Hoskins Commercial State Bank."

*　　*　　*

Walter sat reading the Norfolk Daily News before supper while Jeannine and Fauneil were taking turns practicing the piano. He had finished reading the current news and the editorials and was looking at the ads when Lisetta entered the living room.

"Well, Lisetta, the war has finally led us out of the depression. We'll never see beefsteak at five cents a pound again."

"I hope not. Remember how we struggled to make a living at our little grocery store?"

"Ja, and then selling up and moving to Minnie's farm for a **better life.**

"The economy is better now, but we're still scrimping and saving. Will our farm mortgage ever be paid off?" Walter stood up, hugged her, and smacked her on the lips. "Zettie, I paid off the last of the mortgage today!"

"Hooray! Now you can stop working so hard, and I can spend a bit now and then." Jeannine and Fauneil joined in the excitement. "Can we spend a bit now and then, too?"

"If I gave you each a dollar," answered Walter, "what would you spend it on?"

"A book," answered Fauneil. Jeannine nodded.

* * *

The girls had become interested in reading when Loretta and Engeline, Lisetta's cousins, began giving them books for Christmas and their birthdays. Loretta started them on the Pollyanna series, and Engie on the Nancy Drew mysteries. Reading their own and each other's books gave the girls double the reading material. After both had read the latest Pollyanna book, <u>Pollyanna Grows Up</u>, they talked about how good, honest, sweet, and caring Pollyanna was. She inspired them to become better, and they decided one sunny day to act on her advice.

"You know how Hertha Beilenberg is always so grumpy," Jeannine said. "Let's be like Pollyanna and see if we can make her nicer."

"Good idea!" responded Fauneil. They walked over to the Beilenberg house. Hertha was working in her garden and did not look up when the girls approached.

"Hi, Bertha," said Jeannine sweetly. Bertha did not answer.

"Hi, Bertha!" yelled Fauneil. Still no answer.

"What lovely flowers you have," complimented Jeannine.

"The prettiest in Hoskins," added Fauneil.

"Huh!" responded Hertha. "Watch out there! Don't step on my daisies!" She gave them an angry look and waved them off. The girls ran away.

"What a sourpuss," commented Jeannine.

"Ja, being a *Pollyanna* doesn't work."

The girls had more success playing "Nancy Drew." They had just finished reading The Clue in the Diary. One afternoon they looked through family picture albums, hunting for a clue. They came across a photo of Minnie's family: her parents, looking very strict, her three sisters, and her four brothers. The family were arranged in two rows, the parents and girls seated, and the boys standing behind. Jeannine and Fauneil remembered the names of the girls and could recognize them by age because they were seated oldest to youngest. They studied the youngest brother in the top row, but couldn't match him with a name they had heard.

"I don't like his looks," commented Jeannine.

"Ja, he looks sneaky. Let's ask Mom about him when she gets back from the co-op." In the evening, they showed Lisetta the picture and asked about him.

"His name was Paul. He was the 'bad egg' in the family. He used to buy and sell cattle for other farmers at the auction house in Omaha. The local farmers trusted him with large sums of cash, and Paul took the time to travel 120 miles to Omaha, saving the farmers a day of work. Paul enjoyed these trips because they gave him an opportunity to escape the boredom of farm life. One night he didn't return from Omaha. He simply vamoosed with a large roll of cash."

"You mean he stole the money?"

"Ja. No one ever heard from him again."

"Wow!" exclaimed Fauneil, "our clue was right. He was sneaky!"

*　　*　　*

Chapter VI
Decisions

War News
1944

June 6, 1944 became known as D-Day, the day that the Allies landed on the beaches of France to begin the liberation of Europe. There were five assault divisions: one Canadian, two British, and two American. For the U.S., the worst casualties occurred on Omaha Beach, where the 1st and 29th Divisions, plus special forces, encountered the heaviest opposition by the German forces. The snipers defended their positions from bunkers located on cliffs above the beach landing of the crafts and amphibious tanks. Nearly 3,000 Americans were killed or injured on Omaha Beach.

* * *

D-Day brought the Hoskins community closer to the war. Everyone knew someone whose friend or relative was fighting the war in Europe. Jeannine and Fauneil heard their parents talking about Clarence, Lyle, and Gilbert, three of the sons of Annie, Walter's elder sister.

"Do you think one or perhaps all of Annie's boys were part of the invasion?" asked Lisetta.

"They are certainly in Europe, but who knows where," answered Walter.

* * *

For Jeannine and Fauneil, the war was too remote for concern. They were looking forward to a glorious time to spend at Uncle Emil's farm. Emil had purchased the farm from his mother and father when they moved to the acreage. The farmhouse, which was situated on a hill, was surrounded on three sides by a large covered veranda; two sides looked out to broad cottonwood trees; the third side faced a big barn and oak trees. Behind the barn were buildings for livestock and chickens; beyond them were fields of corn and oats and pastures for grazing. Emil's wife, Berenice, had planted near the house a flower garden, dominated by huge white, pink, and rose peonies. Because the flowers were so numerous, Emil had placed beehives nearby to house the bees, who collected the nectar for themselves and for their keepers. Adjacent to a vegetable garden was a cave, where Berenice stored fruits and vegetables. When Lisetta drove the girls to Emil's farm, she parked on the road near the barn, and they walked up the hill towards the house.

"This is an old house," Lisetta informed them. "It was once the Meritz home for my family on a farm several miles away. It was moved on boards and rollers to this location after Grandpa Getzmer purchased it from my dad. Your father was about your age when this house became the Getzmer home."

"Gosh!" exclaimed Jeannine. "You and Dad lived in the same house!"

"But not at the same time," reminded Fauneil.

After a short visit, Lisetta left, and Emil led the girls upstairs to unpack and get settled in their bedroom. It was the first room at the top of the stairs. "This was your Uncle Ferd's and your dad's bedroom when they lived here," said Emil.

"Is this where Dad saw the ghost?" asked Fauneil.

42

"Ja, but ghosts can't hurt you. Look in all of the rooms up here. You won't find any ghosts."

After the girls had put their clothes into the closet and the dresser, they explored the upstairs. They found some old furniture and two large pictures of reindeer in one of the bedrooms; the rest of the rooms were empty.

"No ghosts," announced Jeannine.

"Boo-ooo-ooo," wailed Fauneil behind a closed door.

"Oh, shut up! Let's go climb those big oak trees down by the barn."

Jeannine climbed one and Fauneil another. The lower limbs of the trees touched each other. The girls pretended that the trees were houses, and they visited each other by stepping back and forth between the trees. The large branches became rooms in their tree houses: living room, dining room, kitchen, and bedrooms. As Fauneil peered out between the leaves of her "second-story bedroom," she spotted a house located adjacent to a group of beehives.

"Look, Jeannine! There's a house that looks deserted. Let's go look for a ghost."

"We better ask Uncle Emil first. Maybe tomorrow we can."

The next morning during breakfast, Uncle Emil asked the girls how they had slept. "Fine," answered Jeannine, untruthfully. The moon had come through the filmy curtains, giving the room an eerie cast. The floor had creaked, and the door had rattled. The girls had hidden under the covers, afraid of seeing a ghost.

"I'm glad you slept well," responded Aunt Berenice. "Old houses, like this one, sometimes make strange noises. You hear them more at night when you're not busy."

After breakfast, the girls followed Uncle Emil around as he did his chores: feeding the hogs, the chickens, and the dog; pitching hay from the barn loft for the milk cows and then milking them one at a time; running the separator; taking the milk and cream to the house, and then cleaning the separator.

"The gathering of the eggs is Berenice's job, but today it's your job, girls," said Uncle Emil. "Grab a basket, and put each egg in carefully so it doesn't break. If a hen is still on her nest, reach under for an egg. You just might find one!"

"Like an Easter egg hunt," offered Fauneil.

"After gathering the eggs, take them into the kitchen and ask your aunt if she is planning to bake, and then help her."

"Okay," said Jeannine. "Say, Uncle Emil, who lives in that house?" She pointed west to the deserted house.

"It used to belong to a family named Pippit, but I own that farm now. Still in the mood for exploring?" The girls nodded. "After you help your aunt, go over and have a look around. It's open."

In the afternoon, Jeannine and Fauneil crossed the field to the deserted house. The screen door hung on one hinge, but the wooden door was stuck firmly in place. Jeannine and Fauneil pushed hard, and it gave way with a sudden jerk. They almost fell onto the floor, which was covered with broken pieces of gray linoleum and shards of glass.

"Let's see what's in these cupboards," suggested Jeannine.

"You look," responded Fauneil. "I'm going to look for ghosts." Jeannine found only some broken pottery in the cupboards.

"Hey, Jeannine, come see what I found!" Jeannine clomped up the stairs.

"Well, what is it?"

"A plastic soldier and paper dolls and some comic strips."

"So?"

"Children must have lived here."

"Okay, okay. We better go."

"Wait. Let's read some of these old comic strips first." The girls sat down on the dirty floor and looked through the strips of Homer Hoopee, Ella Cinders, Blondie and Dagwood, and the Katzenjammer Kids.

That evening at the supper table, Uncle Emil asked if they had found any ghosts in the deserted house. Jeannine laughed and explained that they had only found children's things.

"Oh, those must have been Ralph's and Beverly's things – your cousins," explained Emil. "They lived there during the depression when you were living on your Grandma Meritz's farm."

"Did they see ghosts in the house?" asked Fauneil.

"You, young lady, seem to be extremely interested in the spirit world."

"Spirit world? You mean ghosts?"

"Ja! Ghosts!"

*   *   *

War News
Fall 1944 – March 1945

After D-Day, Hitler declared that a new U-boat (called The Walter) and flying bombs, his new miracle weapons, would turn the tide against the Allies.

The Walter increased underwater speed and could stay submerged longer because of its increased battery power. This was superior to any of the Allies' submarines.

On June 13, 1944, one week after D-Day, the first V-1s (flying bombs) were fired at England. The V-1 missiles could reach a speed of 420 mph and a range of 125 miles. At first, they were launched from sites on the ground; later when the Allies began discovering and bombing the sites, the Germans developed mobile launchers. The V-2s, which were free-flight rockets, were more deadly than the V-1s.

46

They could reach greater speeds and were faster to launch, making it almost impossible for the Allies to locate and destroy them. Thirty-three thousand people in England were killed or injured by 10,500 V-1s and 1,115 V-2s.

The leading rocket scientist was Wernher von Braun, who stayed and worked at Peenemunde, an experimental site on the Baltic Coast until the Soviet advance in March 1945. After surrendering to the Americans, von Braun defected to the U.S., where he continued to work on missiles for the U.S, government, including the NASA rocket to the moon which was launched in 1969.

If German scientists, such as von Braun, had perfected their new technologies earlier in the war, the final outcome might have favored Germany

*   *   *

Fred Feiler, the owner of the Hoskins Lumber Store, came into the co-op to see Walter.

"My wife and I have decided to move to Palo Alto, California to be near our son."

"Sorry to see you go, Fred."

"Well, we'll miss Hoskins. Say, Walt, I might need your help in selling my lumber business. And we're looking for a buyer for our house, as well."

When Walter went home for supper, he relayed the news to Lisetta. "The Feilers are selling their house and moving to California. I know you've always admired that house from the outside. Want to have a look at the inside? I earned enough this summer for a down payment."

"You bet, Walt!"

The two-story house was located on the main street, where the lawns were spacious and the trees tall and beautiful. A red brick fireplace was visible next to a front porch. The first floor had a large living room, a spacious dining room, a modern kitchen, a bedroom, a bath, and a small den. Upstairs were a second bathroom and one very large bedroom, spanning the length of the house.

"This bedroom would be perfect for our three girls," said Lisetta. "Each of them could have a bed of her own, and there's room for both a study area and an entertainment area."

"It seems like the house was designed for our family," agreed Walter. "Let's make an offer."

Lisetta went to bed excited. In her mind, she imagined where she would place her furniture and how she would decorate the rooms. Two days later, Walter came home from the co-op with disappointing news. The Feilers had sold their house to a farmer who had paid cash for it.

"Maybe we can find another house you like, Lisetta."

"There's nothing here. That was the nicest house in Hoskins."

"Well, we weren't meant to have it, Lisetta."

In September, Walter came home with the news that the Pentico farm, northeast of Hoskins, would be offered at an auction sale in November.

"This might be a good opportunity to get a second farm at a good price," he said to Lisetta. "I've earned enough this summer to outbid other bidders, and besides, I'm good at the "bidding game." My buying and selling livestock at the auction house have taught me a lot."

"The bidding is all mumbo-jumbo to me, but you understand it, Walt."

"I figure the farm would sell for about $15,000. I could offer a down payment of twenty percent: $3,000. Of course, if we put our money down on a farm, we can't buy a house as well."

"There's no pretty house in Hoskins to buy right now, Walt. Besides, November is two months off. Let's wait and see what happens."

In October, Walter received a letter from Fred Feiler in Palo Alto, thanking him for helping him to sell his lumber store. Walter read the last paragraph aloud to Lisetta:

Have you thought, Walt, about leaving Hoskins? It is such a   small community for someone with your ambition. The opportunities in business and real estate are numerous here in Palo Alto. Perhaps you should consider a move for the sake of yourself and your family. If you are interested in information about this area, I will gladly send you some material.

"What do you think, Zettie? Hoskins and the Pentico farm or Palo Alto?"

"Fred Feiler is right. You **are** ambitious, Walt. Perhaps he's right about Hoskins, too. Are we stuck in the mud here?"

"Well, I don't see any future for myself at the co-op. I like to be out and about, not working behind a counter."

"In your heart, you're still a farm boy, Walt."

"I know it. I'm the happiest when I'm involved with farming – on the road adjusting farm losses, or helping someone here to sell their farm, or managing a farm for myself or others, like Hertha and Bertha."

"You are, so follow your heart, Walt."

*   *   *

A week later, Minnie stopped at the acreage to visit with Lisetta. "My renter at 1208 Nebraska Avenue is leaving at the end of October," she announced.

"Do you have another renter in mind, Ma?"

"Ja. You and Walt and the girls."

"But his job is here, and rent is cheap in Hoskins."

"Zettie, I'm offering my house to live in rent free. If you keep up the property taxes and pay the insurance on it, I'll be satisfied. It was your home when we lived there together, and you know the neighborhood."

"But you'd be losing rent, Ma."

"No *but*s. Lyle has been getting the farm almost rent free all of these years. I don't need the money, and now it's your turn."

"Thanks for your offer, Ma. I'll talk it over with Walt."

When Lisetta told Walter about Minnie's proposal, he said, "Now we have a third choice: Hoskins, Norfolk, or Palo Alto. It was nice if Minnie, but . . ." He was interrupted.

"No *but*s, Ma said. If we moved to California, it would be devastating for her. She was only forty-three when Dad died, and she carried on with Lyle and me, the farms, and the depression – you know it all, Walt."

"You're right, Lisetta. Minnie deserves to be a major part of our decision. I think that rules out Palo Alto."

"Yes, absolutely. So, you can bid on the Pentico farm in November, whether we move to Norfolk or not."

"You're right, Zettie. Now it's a question of my work and what's best for the family."

"You're unhappy at the co-op. Why not start your own business in Norfolk? Real estate, insurance, and farm management."

"I would need an office, and Norfolk is more expensive."

"The rent would be free in Ma's house, and it's a much nicer house than this one on the acreage. It has a living room and a dining room. You could use either of those for an office until your business gets established."

"There are only two bedrooms, one for us and the other for all three girls."

"Jeannine and Fauneil can sleep in a double bed, and we could put Marleen's youth bed in the same room."

"You're a genius, Zettie. You and Minnie both have the gift of seeing a way to solve a problem."

By the end of November, they had purchased the Pentico farm and were living at 1208 Nebraska Avenue in Norfolk. Walter was working at the dining room table; Marleen was following Lisetta around as she unpacked boxes and arranged their belongings; and Jeannine and Fauneil were trying to adjust to their new school.

Part II
On the Way

Chapter VII
Adjusting to Norfolk

War News – Europe
July, 1944 – May, 1945

After D-Day, the Allied forces began their sweep across Europe:

1944

July 18 – 20	Caen fell, ending the German resistance there.
July 2	Operation Bagration – Soviets moved into Poland.
July 25	Operation Cobra – Allies advanced from Normandy.
August 15	Operation Dragoon – Allies landed in South France.
August 25	Allies liberated Paris
September 15	U.S. troops reached the Siegfried Line.

September 17	*Operation Market Garden – an airborne operation which secured bridges in Holland.*
October 16	*Red Army entered East Prussia.*
November 2	*Canadians took Zeebrugge, Belgium.*
November 23	*French troops liberated Strasbourg.*
December 16	*In a final effort Germans launched The Battle of the Bulge.*
December 26	*Americans were relieved by General Patton's Third Army.*
1945	
January 27	*Soviet troops liberated Warsaw, Poland.*
January 30	*Soviets advanced to the Oder River, 40 miles from Berlin.*
February 13-14	*British and Americans bombed Dresden.*
April 15	*British and Canadians liberated Bergen-Belsen concentration camp.*
April 28	*Mussolini was killed by Italian partisans.*
April 30	*Hitler committed suicide in Berlin.*

May 2   *Soviets took Berlin after 12 days of*
                          house-to-house fighting.

*   *   *

The Allied sweep across Europe was heartening news to Americans. In Norfolk, Nebraska, Walter was beginning to feel better about the changes that were taking place and those that he was creating

"You've regained your spirit for working, Walt," commented Lisetta as she passed by him, concentrating at the dining room table as he worked on an insurance policy for a new customer.

"Ja, the old hard-working pioneer spirit is back. I just needed a change. You know, adjusting to living and working here hasn't been difficult."

Several years after Lisetta's father, Gus, died, Minnie purchased a lot at 1208 Nebraska Avenue and built a house for herself and Lisetta. At the time, Lisetta was attending Norfolk Junior College and was dating Walter, who was living with his parents in Hoskins; so, Norfolk had been an extension of Hoskins. Walter had divided his time between the two communities.

Since their move, Norfolk and Hoskins were again extensions of each other. Walter motored back and forth to visit his farms and those he managed. As a real estate agent, he was building new contacts in Norfolk while retaining those in Hoskins.

St. Paul's Lutheran Church became their spiritual home. It was the home of the early pioneers and had been the "mother" church to Trinity Evangelical in Hoskins. Among the members was Paul Rohrke, whose father had employed Walter at the Hoskins State Bank before the Great Depression. Paul and Walter became good friends. Because Walter had a likeable personality, he soon made new friends with members of the Norfolk Real Estate Association and the Lions Club, which he joined.

Lisetta became reacquainted with members of the St. Paul's Ladies Aid Society. Some of the older members she remembered from the time she had lived here with Minnie. Lisetta and four-year-old Marleen kept each other company at home when Jeannine and Fauneil were at school. Walter and Lisetta had purchased two new special friends for Marleen: Skipper, a fox terrier puppy, and Mitzi, a kitten whom Marleen treated like one of her dolls.

For Jeannine and Fauneil, adjusting to life in Norfolk was a painful experience. They missed all of their delightful spots on the acreage and in Hoskins, as well as their teacher and their classmates. They tried to make new friends at Grant Elementary School, but their classmates had grown up together in the school and already had their own circle of friends.

Walking to and from the Sacred Heart Conservatory of Music on Saturdays for their piano lessons was another difficult adjustment. Hoskins was a quiet village with little traffic. Now the girls had to follow stop lights and signs and look carefully in all directions before crossing a street.

One cold, icy Saturday morning in late March, Jeannine and Fauneil were walking along busy Norfolk Avenue on the way to their piano lessons. They stopped at an intersection and waited on the curb for the traffic to clear. A lady pulled up to the stop sign and motioned the girls to cross. As they stepped off the curb, a pickup truck sped around the corner, knocking down Fauneil and running over her right arm. The driver caught Jeannine's coat on his bumper and dragged her halfway down the block on the snow-covered, cinder-strewn street before stopping.

Marleen was at home, humming to herself as she wheeled Mitzi about in her doll carriage. She stopped, picked up Mitzi, and set her down in a chair. "Wake up, Mitzi! It's time to eat your lunch. Now eat all of those green beans! If you don't, you can't go outside to play." She shook her finger at Mitzi.

Lisetta, who was dusting furniture nearby, smiled. She went out to the front porch and shook out her dust rag. Back inside, she stood, looking out the window at nothing in particular. Suddenly the telephone rang.

"Mrs. Getzmer, I'm calling from the Lutheran Hospital. Your daughters have just been brought here in an ambulance."

"Oh, my God! How are they?"

"Jeannine's legs and thighs are badly scraped, and Fauneil is unconscious."

"I'll be right there." She called and left a message for Walt, bundled up Marleen, and walked through the backyard and across the alley to the hospital. When she arrived, Fauneil had regained consciousness.

"Look at my arm, Mom!" she said, pointing to a very swollen limb, which was already turning shades of black and blue.

"Miraculously, the arm isn't broken," said the attending doctor, "but watch Fauneil for concussion; she received a bad blow to her head." He handed Lisetta a bottle of antiseptic solution, saying, "Jeannine will need to have her abrasions washed daily with this; however, some of the pieces of cinder are quite deep and may have to remain under her skin."

"Mom, we waited at the intersection, but a lady motioned us across," said Jeannine apologetically.

"Don't worry. It wasn't your fault. Thank heavens you're both alive."

The accident was written up in The Norfolk Daily News. When Jeannine and Fauneil returned to school, they received some attention from their classmates, especially Fauneil, whose arm kept changing colors from black and blue to purple and finally to yellow. The attention was short-lived, and Fauneil was soon ignored again.

*   *   *

War News
May 7, 1945

The Germans last stand had been in the Ardennes. The Allied air and ground forces were hampered by the heavy

58

snowfall and the lack of fuel. However, the Soviets, who were used to winter warfare, pursued from the East towards Berlin. When Allied bombing resumed, the British by night and the Americans by day, Berlin and Dresden were reduced to rubble. The destruction of Dresden, the city which was beloved by the Germans because of its Baroque architecture, broke the spirit of any citizens who were still loyal to the Axis. Dresden was not only bombed relentlessly for two days, but set on fire so that only burnt-out shells of buildings remained. Many residents died from bombs or were unable to escape from the raging fires.

On May 7, Germany unconditionally surrendered.

On May 8, Europe celebrated VE Day (Victory in Europe).

*   *   *

The teachers at Grant School discussed the meaning of the surrender in the classroom. At recess time, the children whooped and ran about and acted silly. At the end of recess, the teachers instructed them to form a circle, hold hands, and sing the patriotic songs, "My Country 'tis of Thee" and "America the Beautiful."

*   *   *

By the last week in May, summer vacation started for Jeannine and Fauneil. They looked forward to spending several weeks with Minnie on her farm.

Minnie was busy making chokecherry jam when Lisetta drove them there. The next day, Minnie put the girls to work in her kitchen, peeling peaches and cutting them into halves before she put them into jars, poured on the sauce she had prepared, and closed the jars with rubber-lined lids. Each day, Minnie chose a different fruit or vegetable to can, instructing the girls how to peel, cut, or dice.

In the afternoon, the girls were free to play. They usually walked up Minnie's steep lane and then crossed the road to their Uncle Lyle's farm to play with their cousins, Lyla and Lon. They enjoyed jumping in the corncrib. This required climbing up steps inside the bin to the top and then leaping down into the shelled corn, which covered them to the waist. After crawling out of the corn, they repeated the action.

Near the fields, there was a grove of large trees, where they played tag or hide-and-go-seek. On one occasion, Lon sneaked out of the house one of Lyle's cigars and a box of matches. The four youths sat leaning against tree trunks and passed around a lit cigar, taking turns puffing it. Although they didn't inhale, the smokey air made them sick, and Lon soon stomped the cigar butt out.

The favorite game for the girls was "playing Cherry Ames." All of the girls had been reading the Cherry Ames series, which was popular because of the war. They used the fruit and vegetable cellar in an underground cave as their hospital when they played "Cherry Ames, Army Nurse."

The girls decided on the needed supplies and sent Lon to round them up: two blankets for a gurney and an operating table, a tweezer for a forceps, toothpicks for needles, and a plastic knife for a scalpel. While Lon went to the house to fetch the items, the girls gathered a bucket of water from an outdoor pump, a big stick for a crutch, large leaves for bandages, and the dog's empty bowl, which they filled with dirt to be mixed with water to make mud for a salve.

When Lon returned, he brought his younger brother, Lane, to help him carry the items. "Good," said Lyla. "Lane, you can be one of the soldiers." Lyla assigned the roles for the game according to seniority. "I'll be the doctor; Jeannine will be Cherry Ames; Fauneil, the corpsman; Lon, soldier 1; and Lane, soldier 2."

"Let's begin," said Cherry Ames. "The cave is the hospital – girls, inside; boys, outside on the battlefield. Everyone, take your places!"

"We're ready," said the doctor. "Corpsman, bring in the first wounded soldier." Fauneil walked outside where Lon and Lane were sitting on the steps. She led Lon, who was hobbling with a stick, into the cave and announced, "This soldier has a wounded leg."

"Get up on this gurney," ordered Nurse Cherry, pointing to a blanket draped over a sack of potatoes. Lon climbed onto the sack and held out one leg. "Summon the doctor," the nurse said to the corpsman. Lyla moved forward from inside the cave. "Nurse, pull up his uniform so I can examine the wound." Jeannine pulled up the leg of Lon's overalls. "It needs stitching," announced the doctor. Nurse Ames handed her a toothpick to use to close the wound. "Now apply an ointment and a bandage." Jeannine smeared mud on Lon's leg and stuck a large leaf on top. "You're all done," stated the corpsman to the soldier. "Bring in the next soldier," ordered Nurse Ames.

Fauneil and Lon exited the cave and carried Lane into the

operating room. "He's seriously wounded!" said the corpsman excitedly. "Fetch the doctor immediately!" Lyla came forward. "Put him on the operating table," she ordered, pointing to a blanket on the step. "Get the plasma going," she ordered Nurse Cherry. Jeannine sprinkled water on Lane's arm. "Swab the area on his belly." The nurse lifted Lane's shirt and poured water onto his belly. "Ooh, that's cold," complained Lane.

The operation began. The doctor asked for each item, and the nurse responded: scalpel (a plastic knife), forceps (a tweezer), needle (a toothpick), salve (mud), bandage (leaf). "Now," said Lyla – she was interrupted.

"I'm tired of this game," complained Lane. "Me, too," added Lon. "Let's go jump in the corncrib again." They left.

"Just like boys to leave us to clean up this mess," complained Lyla. "Well, let's get it done before Mom sees it."

Chapter VIII
Awaiting the Outcome

War News in the Pacific
February 11, 1944 – April 1, 1945

With General MacArthur as commander, the Allied forces "island-hopped" as they fought their way closer to Japan.

1944

February 11 U.S. landed in the Marshall Islands.

February 17 Americans bombed the Japanese naval base in the Caroline Islands, destroying 200,000 tons of shipping.

March 4 Operations began in Burma.

March 7 Japanese launched an offensive in Burma, aimed at India.

Mar. 30 Imphal, India was besieged by the Japanese.

April 18 Japan launched a new offensive in central China.

June 19 U.S. landed in the Mariana Islands.

June 20 Japanese suffered heavy aircraft losses in the Battle of the Philippines.

August 3 Mjitkyina, Burma was taken by the Allies.

October 20	U.S. landed in the Philippines.
October 23-26	Japanese suffered heavy losses in the Philippines, where they first used Kamikaze aircraft.
January 22	The Burma Road (the supply route to Southern China) was reopened by the Allies.
February 19	U.S. landed on the island of Iwo Jima.
March 9-10	U.S. bombed Tokyo, killing 100,000 people.
April	Americans landed on Okinawa.

* * *

Back in Norfolk, Walter and Lisetta were busy with their typical summer duties. Walter, who was still working as a hail adjustor, was alternating between two weeks "on the road" and two weeks at home. In that way, he could earn more money and still keep his business in Norfolk going. He now had an office in downtown Norfolk, but he did not have enough business yet to hire a secretary, so Lisetta and Marleen walked to Walt's office once a week when Walt was gone. Lisetta attended to the mail, answered the phone, and did a little filing. Marleen scribbled on paper and colored. When they were finished, Lisetta purchased some baked goods at the bakery and then stopped in at the soda fountain in the drugstore to treat Marleen.

"Have you been busy this summer?" Lisetta asked the young lady behind the counter.

"Yes. Some of the soldiers are already returning from Europe. Are any of your relatives coming home?"

"My husband's three nephews – all from the same family."

"Not all families have been that fortunate."

"Walt still has his nephew, Leslie, fighting in the Pacific."

"Gruesome fighting there in those islands, and now in Japan itself."

"Ja. Leslie is lucky not to be in combat. He was sent to the military school for languages in Monterey, California to learn Japanese, and he is now an interpreter."

"The Japanese don't seem to be willing to give up. Who knows how long it will be before the war in the Pacific is over!

*   *   *

War News
August 6, 1945

The war in the Pacific continued with the siege of Japan and the Great Yokohama Air Raid on May 29th, killing 8,000 people in one hour. President Roosevelt died during his fourth term in office and was succeeded by President Harry S. Truman. It became Truman's decision whether or not to use the new weapon, the atomic bomb, which had been created and tested in New Mexico. He chose to use it, thereby saving the lives of Allies rather than those of the Japanese.

On August 6th, the U.S. dropped its first atomic bomb on Hiroshima. In spite of the warning to Japan that the U.S. had a second bomb, the Japanese still did not surrender. The second bomb was dropped on August 9th in Nagasaki. Horrible devastation and severe loss of lives occurred. On September 2nd, the Japanese surrendered aboard the USS Missouri, and President Truman announced that the war was over.

*   *   *

In the fall of 1945, Fauneil was a sixth-grader at Grant, and Jeannine started the seventh grade at St. Paul's Lutheran Parochial School in preparation for her confirmation at the end of the eighth grade. There were two classrooms at St. Paul's, one for grades one through four and another for grades five through eight. The lower grades met in a building that had been built in 1883; the upper grades in a building which had been the second church building of the congregation. Its wooden frame was topped by a high-pitched roof; colored glass Gothic windows were located on the sides of the structure; and double wooden doors were in the front of building. The students entered a cloakroom that had formerly been the vestibule of the church and then walked through a second pair of doors into the classroom.

When Jeannine entered on her first day, she saw Mr. Krenz, the teacher, standing in front of the blackboards across the room. He was a tall, balding, slightly pot-bellied man dressed in a gray pin-striped suit, a white shirt, and a black tie. With a stern voice and visage, he assigned seats and stated the rules for behavior.

Jeannine had been accustomed to a multi-grade classroom at the Hoskins parochial school and adjusted easily to the study-recitation technique Mr. Krenz used. But the main anxiety for her was Mr. Krenz's high expectation of performance. He kept a notebook of questions missed by students during recitation; those who answered incorrectly had to stay in during recess and write the question and answer ten times each. Jeannine studied hard, striving for perfection, as did Fauneil a year later when she started at St. Paul's.

Although Mr. Krenz was extremely strict, he was genuinely interested in each of his pupils. When he discovered, through the students' daily singing of hymns, that Jeannine had a beautiful voice, he encouraged Walter and Lisetta to start her on voice lessons. When he observed that Fauneil loved literature, he encouraged them to introduce her to the public library.

*   *   *

The winter of 1946-1947 was severe. Before Lisetta sent the girls to school, she gave them hot cereal with hot milk and coffee to drink. She made sure that they were well bundled up: long stockings, sweaters, coats, mittens (two pairs each), woolen caps, and shawls around their faces. When the snow wasn't too deep, the girls rode their bicycles the mile-long trek to school. On the way home, they engaged in a contest to see who could get the farthest up a long, steep hill before getting off and pushing her bike.

Throughout the winter, six-year-old Marleen suffered from tonsillitis. Finally, Lisetta and Walter decided that her tonsils and adenoids had to come out. They remembered that when Jeannine and Fauneil had had theirs out, they had experienced discomfort, but that was all.

At first Marleen seemed to be healing, but ten days after the operation, she began to hemorrhage. Dr. Brauer came immediately to the house and tried to stop the bleeding, but it continued sporadically into the evening. Finally, at one o-clock, he sent the family to bed but remained at Marleen's bedside throughout the night. In the morning, Lisetta found Dr. Brauer sitting by the bed, with the head of the bed now set up on blocks. Marleen lay there like a corpse, pale and still. Suddenly she sat up and began to wretch.

"Get a basin!" ordered Dr. Brauer. Lisetta returned with the basin just in time to catch an orange-sized lump of brown clotted blood.

"She'll be alright now," said the doctor.

"Thank God you were here, Dr. Brauer."

"Well, I brought her into this world. I wouldn't want to lose her over a tonsillectomy.

* * *

By late March, Marleen was feeling spunky enough to engage in her favorite after-school activity – playing school. Her play school consisted of wooden boxes which she brought out of the tool room in the basement and set up in the large, warm furnace room. Skipper and Mitzi were her students for a music lesson. She set each "student" on top of a box, blew a note on a pitch pipe, and directed them to sing. Skipper jumped immediately down from his box and slunk off behind the furnace. Mitzi took it in her stride and remained on her box.

"Skipper always runs off," Marleen complained to Fauneil, who was dancing to a phonograph record across the room.

"The pitch pipe probably hurts his ears," answered Fauneil. "It's about suppertime," she added. "Let's go upstairs."

*   *   *

Chapter IX
More Decisions

During supper in the kitchen, the telephone rang, and Walter went into the dining room to answer it.

"That was Art Post," he said. "He's coming here from Omaha next week to talk with me about the Bureau."

"Not more time away from home this summer, Walt," complained Lisetta. A week later, after Mr. Post's visit, Walter revealed the reason for Art's trip to Norfolk.

"Art wants me to be the new Regional Manager for the Omaha Rain and Hail Bureau."

"What would that mean?" asked Lisetta.

"An excellent salary, an important position, and a move to Omaha. If I don't accept the position now, they won't offer it again. I have to let Art know by the end of the week."

"Let's mull it over before we discuss it," suggested Lisetta.

At bedtime, she prayed that Walt would make the right decision for the entire family. On Friday evening, Lisetta and Walter had their discussion after the three girls had gone to bed.

"Let's discuss the good points and then the bad points of a move to Omaha," suggested Lisetta.

"O.K. The good points: a more prestigious job for me, more pay, more management, less travel 'on the road,' better education and music opportunities for the girls, and probably a bigger and better house for you, Lisetta, and the family."

"Yes," responded Lisetta. "Next, the bad points: We would have adjustments to make. For you, Walt, a new job; for the girls, a change of schools and of music teachers; for all of us, a change of church and a change from a small city to a very large one."

"I'm afraid I'll make the wrong decision," admitted Walter.

"Walt, if we move to Omaha, our family wouldn't be the only ones affected. The tenants on our farms would be as well, and the tenants on the farms you manage for clients. Bertha Beilenberg would be devastated."

"That's right. I need to consider that."

"Why don't you take a drive into the countryside tomorrow and visit with a few tenants about it?"

*   *   *

The next day, Walter stopped at three different farms on his route. His last stop was at the Fred Thomas farm. When he pulled into the yard, Fred was just coming from the area of the windmill.

"Hi there, Walt. What brings you out here today?"

"Something I would like to get your opinion on."

"Oh?"

"I've been offered a pretty big position as the manager for the Rain and Hail Bureau in   Omaha."

"How could you manage your farms here, Walt? Omaha is 240 miles round-trip."

"Well, I'd have to make the drive less often and probably on a weekend."

"Leave your family at home? Drive home late?"

"I have quite a few farm clients. I guess I would have to stay in Norfolk overnight, or I could turn the farms over to another farm manager to look after."

"Walt, you said you wanted my opinion. Well, I say *no* to both of   those ideas. And you're forgetting what you'd be giving up: the sunshine and fresh air, the smell of the alfalfa, and seeing the cattle grazing in the pasture. To me, that's worth more than a big desk in an office."

Walter nodded, shook Fred's hand and said, "Thanks. I'll let you know what I decide."

*   *   *

When Walter returned from his drive, he said to Lisetta, "I'm still a farm boy at heart. Being cooped up in an office all day wouldn't make me happy. What do you think, Lisetta?"

"I'm a farm girl, too. It would be difficult for me to adjust to big city life. Let's see what the girls think about it." They called the girls into the living room and explained the situation.

Jeannine said, "I don't want to go to a great big high school next year." Fauneil said, "I don't want to leave Sacred Heart for a new music teacher." Marleen said, "Skipper and Mitzi couldn't go outside to play in a big city."

"Decided!" exclaimed Walter. "The Getzmer family stays!"

*   *   *

War News
1946 – 1950

Throughout the war and afterwards, changes in locations were affecting millions of people. After the war, geography and political enclaves were re-structured. The country of Germany was split down the middle, and Berlin was divided into four zones: the American, the Soviet (the largest of the four), the British, and the French zones. The country of Poland was located 100 miles to the west. Russia absorbed the countries of Lithuania, Latvia, Moldavia, and a section of Finland.

*In 1948, Israel was founded by the Jews of Palestine.

*In 1947, India and Pakistan gained independence from Britain.

*In 1946, the U.S. granted independence to the Philippines, but retained some of its military bases there.

A new struggle for world dominance was beginning between East and West.

*   *   *

During the summer of 1948, Walter did not go "on the road," He resigned from the Omaha Rain and Hail Bureau. For his office in downtown Norfolk, he hired a secretary who answered the phone, attended to the mail, dealt with the insurance policies, and created a good system of filing. Walter could be out of doors to his heart's delight, visiting farms and selling real estate.

Lisetta was happier, too; she no longer had to endure the loneliness when Walter was gone, and the burden of the family was no longer hers alone throughout the summer months. Because the older girls had their "noses in books" during summer vacation, Marleen became Lisetta's main companion.

* * *

As Jeannine and Fauneil were leaving for the library one Monday morning to return books and check out new ones for the week, Lisetta reminded them that it was "wash day" and to be back in time to hang up clothes on the lines in the backyard.

At ten o-clock, Lisetta said to Marleen, "Where are those girls!"

"They'll be home soon with an armful of books, Mom. Let me hang up the clothes."

"You're a little short yet, honey."

"I can do it. I'll take out a kitchen chair to stand on."

Lisetta carried the heavy basket out to the clotheslines and gave Marleen a lesson in hanging clothes: hang shirts by the shirttails, dresses by the shoulders, pants by the waist, handkerchiefs in groups of three by the corners. "Leave room for the underwear on the inner lines," added Lisetta.

"Ja, I don't want the Salter boys next door to see my panties," answered Marleen.

"When you get done, you can help me give Skipper his bath with the wash water."

Jeannine and Fauneil returned just after Skipper had had his bath. "Look how pink Skipper's skin gets when he has a bath," said Marleen to Jeannine.

"I'll bet he didn't appreciate that hot water," said Jeannine.

"It's not too hot for him. Look at his feet. They're clean enough to kiss." Marleen kissed the bottom of one of Skipper's feet.

"Is he your *feetheart?*" asked Fauneil.

"*Feetheart?*"

"Ja. He's not a person, so he can't be your sweetheart. So, he must be your *feetheart.*"

"Ja, I love my little *feetheart.*" Marleen hugged Skipper before setting him down. He shook himself and scampered up the stairs.

"Help me in the kitchen," said Lisetta to the older girls. "Your dad will be home soon for noon dinner."

When Walter arrived at 12:15, he turned on the radio in the kitchen to listen to the cattle and hog market as he ate. Until he turned off the radio, the girls had to be quiet.

"That was a delicious pork roast, Lisetta," he praised her, "and there's plenty left over for supper."

"Thanks, Walt." Lisetta had selected a roast large enough for leftovers for the family and possibly an afternoon visitor. Sure enough, about 2:00 p.m., a hobo knocked on the back door.

"Good afternoon, Ma'am. Could I mow your lawn or pull some weeds in exchange for a meal?"

"Yes. Pull those weeds by the garage and put them into the garbage can," she answered with a smile. *He's young*, thought Lisetta. *Probably another soldier who can't find a job.* Lisetta had the hot leftovers waiting for him when he had finished weeding. He ate quickly and handed Lisetta his empty plate, saying "Thank you, Ma'am. That was so good. I'll be on my way."

"Good luck!" said Lisetta. As he was walking away, she was thinking: *That was the third young man I've fed since last Monday. I wonder how they know to come here instead of the neighbor's house. Maybe they have some sort of sign that I don't recognize.*

*   *   *

War News
1945 – 1952

During the war and afterwards, many survivors, both military and civilian, suffered from homelessness, deportation, loss of family, starvation, and trauma.   In the spring of 1945, Germany was flooded with refugees fleeing from the Red Army.   Soldiers and ex-POWs returned home to find their houses in rubble or their loved ones who were dead.   Men drifted from city to city, becoming an army of uniformed tramps, living on the streets.

Five million Soviet citizens had been deported (kidnapped) and sent west to become slave laborers. During the war, some of the captured Russian soldiers were given the choice of fighting for Germany or serving as laborers in the concentration camps.   After the war, those who had fought for Germany were sent back to Russia and treated as traitors and sentenced to gulags.

Throughout Europe, the plight of the survivors included bereavement for lost family, hopelessness for the future, and for some war criminals facing trials, such as the Nuremberg Trials in Germany, imprisonment or death.

* * *

Lisetta was in the kitchen and was considering what she was going to fix for supper since the homeless soldier had eaten the leftovers from the noon dinner.   Marleen ran into the kitchen and interrupted her thoughts.

   "Mom, I can't find Mitzi anywhere."

Lisetta responded with one of her usual suggestions: "Ask Fauneil to help you look."

Fauneil suggested that they look first in the furnace room, where Mitzi often stayed curled up on the wooden box after the "music lesson." Mitzi was still asleep when the girls found her there.

"You're supposed to return these boxes to Dad's tool room when you're through playing," Fauneil scolded her.

"I know I am," answered Marleen as she picked up Mitzi, leaving Fauneil to return the boxes. As soon as Fauneil lifted "Mitzi's box" from the cement floor, a huge centipede scurried across the floor on its "hundred" legs. The girls screamed and ran up the stairs to safety.

"What was that all about?" asked Lisetta. Fauneil responded: "A huge centipede was under Mitzi's box while Mitzi was fast asleep. It could have crawled up my leg when I lifted up the box. Ugh! I hate those things."

That evening, Lisetta reminded Walter about the infestation of the centipedes in the basement, and Walter promised to spray the basement on Saturday with DDT.

* * *

Chapter X
Jeannine

A month after Walter had sprayed the basement for centipedes, Jeannine began to feel ill. Lisetta drove her to see Dr. Brauer, who took a blood sample and found that Jeannine's blood counts were very low. He prescribed Chloromycetin, a new drug designed to prevent the growth of bacteria. He asked Lisetta, "Has Jeannine been around chemicals?"

"Walt sprayed the basement with DDT to kill the centipedes, but Jeannine doesn't go down there anymore to play. Only Fauneil and Marleen do."

"Bring her back in a week, Lisetta, and I'll test her blood again to check her blood counts. In the meantime, start her right away on the Chloromycetin."

Shortly after taking the medication, Jeannine developed a sore throat and headache, followed by diarrhea and nausea. When she developed a high temperature, Lisetta took her again to Dr. Brauer, who ordered a battery of blood tests and found that Jeannine had agranulocytosis, a severe shortage of white cells, leaving her highly susceptible to all kinds of infection. Dr. Brauer gave Lisetta a list of instructions to follow: keep Jeannine isolated and in bed; no school or visitors; discontinue the medication; keep her on a diet of liver once a day and beef broth several times a day; go to Romans Meat Packing for fresh beef blood, and then steam it only, no boiling.

Several days later, Lisetta called Dr. Brauer and reported that Jeannine was running a fever of 104 degrees, and her throat was so red and swollen, she could barely swallow the broth.

"I don't like the looks of this," he said after examining Jeannine at home. "I'd like Doctor Schenken, a pathologist at Methodist Hospital in Omaha, to examine her. Can you and Walt drive her there?" Lisetta nodded.

"I'll call Dr. Schenken and set up an emergency consultation for tomorrow. I'm sure he will want to do a bone marrow test."

"Will it be painful for Jeannine?"

"I'm afraid so, but it will give us a lot of valuable information."

*   *   *

The two-and-a-half-hour drive to Omaha the following day was a silent one. Covered with blankets, Jeannine lay on pillows in the backseat. Her throat was too sore to speak, and Lisetta and Walter were lost in their own thoughts, afraid of the doctor's findings.

After a series of blood tests and the bone marrow test, Dr. Schenken addressed the three of them. "Jeannine does not have leukemia, as Doctor Brauer suspected; instead, she has had a severe reaction to the Chloromycetin. We've been seeing a lot of complications, even deaths, from that new drug." Lisetta turned white.

"There's another new drug called Pentnucleotide, which I've found helpful in some cases, and I'd like to put Jeannine on it."

"Is that our best choice for a cure?" asked Walter.

"The only choice. There is no other drug which can reverse the effects of the Chloromycetin." Doctor Schenken addressed Jeannine: "You'll have to be brave, young lady. The solution is very thick and requires a large needle for injection, and you'll need injections several times a day."

"It looks like I don't have any other choice," whispered Jeannine hoarsely.

On the way home, Lisetta broke the silence. "Jeannine's asleep. This has been a frightful day for her. Walt, why do you suppose they would allow a drug like Chloromycetin on the market?"

"I don't know, but look at vaccines. Most people are saved by them, but a few have severe reactions to them."

"Oh, Walt, suppose Jeannine doesn't respond well to Pentnucleotide."

"It's out of our hands, Lisetta. But not God's. All we can do is pray." Walter became silent again. In his prayer for Jeannine, he included a prayer of supplication for himself. His heart told him that the DDT he had sprayed had started this whole set of circumstances.

*   *   *

Before settling down to sleep that evening, Jeannine went to the bathroom, washed up, and brushed her teeth. Coming back into the bedroom, she pulled up the shades at the windows. The moon was full and bright. She climbed into bed and lay there quietly, enjoying the beauty of the moonlight streaming into the room. At first, she listened to the sounds of the night: the ticking of the clock on the bureau, the rustling of the branches of a dried bush against the siding of the house, the meowing of a cat outside. Then her thoughts turned to herself: her sore throat, headache, and exhaustion; her loneliness and depression; her fear of the future, of Death. She finally fell into a fitful sleep.

Jeannine awoke to the clock in the living room striking two. At first, she was aware only of her own breathing. Then she sensed that she was not alone. An entity was present, a moonlit form by her bedside. Her heart was thumping loudly, but she heard the being communicate: "What are you afraid of, Jeannine?"

"Everything – pain, the future, death."

"Jeannine, have faith." Jeannine felt a soft, tender touch, like a kiss of moonlight. The silvery form expanded until it filled the entire room. When the room could hold it no longer, it became the moonlight.

*   *   *

Everybody tried to help Jeannine to recover. Aunt Lisetta Bech, who had become a practical nurse, came several times a day, to administer the painful shots. Dr. Brauer made house calls to check on Jeannine. Walter spent time in the evenings with Jeannine. Lisetta prepared liver and beef broth. Marleen drew pictures to cheer up Jeannine. Fauneil acted as messenger between home and school.

"How is your sister?" asked Miss Schini when Fauneil went to her room at the end of the school day to get Jeannine's Latin assignment.

"Maybe a little better, thank you."

Fauneil's next stop was to see Miss Durkop, the sophomore English teacher, who handed her a copy of The Mountain Men.

"Have Jeannine read the first chapter of *The Song of Hugh Glass* by John Jacob Neihardt," she said and handed the book to Fauneil.

"Oh, Nebraska's most famous poet," remarked Fauneil. Miss Durkop raised her eyebrows. "I like to read a lot," said Fauneil.

"Well, you would like this. It's about a mountain man who gets mauled in the wilderness by a grizzly bear and is left for dead by his companions." Miss Durkop opened to the first page of the poem and explained the iambic pentameter meter to Fauneil.

"Explain that to your sister," she said, "and tell her to get well soon."

When Fauneil arrived home, the house was in turmoil. Jeannine's thigh was badly swollen from an infection caused by the huge needle that was needed for the Pentnucleotide solution. Minnie had called to find out how Jeannine was. She blamed her sister, (Aunt Lisetta) for not boiling the needles long enough. Aunt Lisetta had hurt feelings when Lisetta relayed the message. Doctor Brauer had come to the house to lance Jeannine's wound, extract the pus, and apply a dressing. While there, he had asked Lisetta if she was well and had said, "You look thin and tired, Lisetta. Try to get more rest."

How, thought Lisetta, *I'm constantly preparing beef broth.*

* * *

When supper was over, she said to Walter, "I'm going to bed early."

"Good," he said. "I'll go in and spend some time with Jeannine." When Walter entered Jeannine's bedroom, she was gloomily staring at The Mountain Men, lying open on her bed.

"I don't know why we have to read this old junk," she complained. Walter peeked over her shoulder.

"Ah, *The Song of Hugh Glass*. I loved that story when I was in high school. Imagine Hugh Glass having to crawl back to civilization alone."

"But it's just a story, Dad."

"Ja, but mountain men like him really did live in this area. They were tough, almost wild men, who struggled each day with the wilderness."

"The land belonged to the Indians then, didn't it?"

"To the Indians and the buffalo, before the homesteaders came. There's a terrific description of a huge stampeding buffalo herd in the story."

"You remember that?"

"Sure do. It's a story worth remembering. Hugh's legs were so badly injured that he had to crawl, but he didn't give in to self-pity. He figured if he was going to die, he was going to die trying." Walter picked up the book. "How far have you read?" Jeannine pointed to the spot. "Lie back, Jeannine, and let me read some of it to you:

> Now when the night wore in middle swoon,
> The crawler, roused from stupor, was aware
> Of some strange alteration in the air.
> To breathe became an act of conscious will.
> The starry waste was ominously still.
> The far-off kiote's yelp came sharp and clear
> As though a tunnel in the atmosphere –
> A ponderable, resonating mass.
> The limp leg dragging on the sun-dried grass
> Produced a sound unnaturally loud.

"Can't you picture that? Alone out under the stars. The only sounds you hear are a coyote's yelp and your leg dragging on the grass."

"Ja, Dad, I can picture it. My leg is throbbing right now."

Walter continued:

> Crouched, panting, Hugh looked up but saw no cloud.
> An oily film seemed spread upon the sky
> Now dully staring as the open eye
> Of one in fever. Gasping, choked with thirst –"

Jeannine reached over for her glass of water.

A week later, Dr. Brauer stood at Jeannine's bedside with the results of the latest blood sample. Walter and Lisetta were present.

"Good news, Jeannine, you're out of the woods and on the way to complete recovery." Jeannine breathed a sigh of relief. She turned towards her parents. "Are you proud of me?" she asked. Lisetta nodded with tears in her eyes. "You bet," answered Walter. "Like Hugh Glass, you just kept on struggling."

*   *   *

Several weeks later, when Jeannine had returned to school for the remainder of the year, Walter resumed his usual evening pattern, reading the newspaper. He was shocked by the editorials, which were about the plight of the Jews during the war and the descriptions that the American soldiers had brought home.

"Lisetta, you have to read these descriptions of the holocaust. Our heritage is German, and I've always been proud of that, but what the Germans did to the Jews is unbelievable."

"Did the citizens really know what was going on?"

"They must have. There were 28 concentration camps throughout Germany, and 8 extermination camps (death camps) in neighboring countries. I think that Jeannine and Fauneil are old enough to learn about this type of cruelty. They should know what happened."

"You're right, Walt. They should know, but not now. Not after this year of suffering that Jeannine has just been through. They can learn about it later. History will remain."

War News
1933 - 1945

The Holocaust

In 1939, there were over 9,000,000 Jews in Europe, including over 500,000 in Germany. As early as 1933 in Germany, the Nuremberg Laws were passed, which stripped the Jews of their citizenship. In 1938, Jewish businesses, cemeteries, and synagogues were attacked. Curfews, rationing (food, clothing, and fuel), identity cards, censorship, restricted movements, forced removal from homes, banishment from schools and public places.

In 1939, Jews were rounded up and forced into ghettos or deported to concentration camps. In the concentration camps, they were separated by those healthy enough to work and those who were not: children, disabled, elderly, homosexuals. In addition to the Jews, the "un-accept-ibles" were the communists and the Roma (gypsies).

By 1945, six million Jews in the camps and an estimated five million outside the camps had died from starvation or disease, or had been put to death in gas chambers, or had succumbed during the death marches towards the end of the war. Twenty-eight concentration camps and eight extermination camps were in existence. Seven sites of mass killings were discovered by the Allies in Russia, Poland, and Romania in1945.

After the war, the Allies held the Nuremberg Trials to convict and punish top military of war crimes. For years, Israeli intelligence hunted down Nazi war criminals. However, the majority of the perpetrators were not apprehended. Manh had escaped to Argentina.

*   *   *

Chapter XI
The Recital

In the fall of 1949, Jeannine was a junior in high school and Fauneil a sophomore. They were both involved in musical groups at the high school, Jeannine in the Concert Choir and the Choraliers, and Fauneil in Orchestra and piano accompaniment for the Concert Choir and the Choraliers. In addition, they were still studying music privately at the Sacred Heart Conservatory of Music.

The girls rang the bell at the Sacred Heart Priory. A nun in a black habit answered the bell and then led them to the top floor of the school building, where Sister Aquinata's music studio was located.

"We'll begin with your piano lesson, Fauneil," said Sister Aquinata.

Fauneil began with major and minor scales and arpeggios, and a Czerny exercise, followed by a Bach two-part invention, a Beethoven sonata, a Chopin etude, and Ernest Seitz's "Butterfly Waltz." As she played, Sister Aquinata did not often interrupt her with comments. Instead, she filled out an evaluation sheet, with a maximum of 12 points for a perfect evaluation: two for technique, 1 ½ for Czerny studies, 1 ½ for Bach studies, 2 for interpretation, 2 for application (practice), and 1 for sight-reading. Sister Aquinata placed the first page of a Brahms rhapsodie on the music rack for Fauneil to sight-read. She marked the score and handed the sheet to Fauneil, who looked for her total: 11 ¾ ; she had dropped ¼ point in the Bach studies.

"I'll have to work harder on the Bach next week," said Fauneil.

"Yes," agreed the sister. "Practice each hand separately and then together. And keep your fingernails short!"

Following Jeannine's piano lesson, Sister Aquinata gave her a voice lesson. Seated at the keyboard, the sister took Jeannine through her vocal exercises, instructing her as she sang. The voice lesson continued with Fauneil seated at the keyboard to accompany Jeannine as she sang an 18th century Italian piece, an aria from The Messiah, and a song based on Elizabeth Barret Browning's "Sonnet 43" in Sonnets from the Portuguese:

> How do I love thee? Let me count the ways.
> I love thee to the depth and breadth and height
> My soul can reach, when feeling out of sight
> For the ends of Being and ideal Grace.
> I love thee to the level of every day's
> Most quiet need, by sun and candlelight.
> I love thee freely, as men strive for Right;
> I love thee purely, as they turn from Praise.
> I love thee with the passion put to use
> In my old griefs, and with my childhood's faith.
> I love thee with a love I seemed to lose
> With my lost saints – I love thee with the breath,
> Smiles, tears of all my life! – and if God choose,
> I shall but love thee better after death.

As Fauneil accompanied, she felt a lump growing in her throat from the beauty of the music, the text, and Jeannine's voice. When Jeannine finished, Fauneil sat still, thinking to herself how glorious it would be to someday experience the kind of love that the Brownings had felt for each other.

"I wish I could sing like Jeannine," she said to Sister Aquinata.

"Both of you girls have your own special musical gifts," she answered. "Be thankful for your own talents." She paused. "Plan to spend extra time with me after your lessons next week. We need to plan your graduation recital for next year."

The following week, she warned them that the recital would take many hours of practice to prepare for it and would involve a great deal of nervous pressure. Then she explained the details of the recital and the requirements for graduation from the conservatory: extra studies in music theory and music history, in addition to performing difficult music in front of a large audience. She added that Theresa Wilson, another of her students, was ready for graduation, and the program would include her.

Towards the end of the discussion, she elicited their responses for the details of the recital: the date, Sunday evening in early December; the place, the Norfolk Auditorium (there would be two Steinway grands on the stage, along with flowers and plants; the performers would wear long gowns); printed programs would be handed out to the audience; advertising for the concert would include posters, flyers, and an announcement in The Norfolk Daily News. Sister Aquinata addressed Jeannine: "You were so ill this last year. Do you think you would be up to the extra work and the pressure?"

"Yes," she answered. "If Fauneil can do it, I can."

       *   *   *

For a year, Jeannine and Fauneil spent many extra hours in the living room practicing. Fortunately, they had a beautiful instrument on which to practice. (Minnie had given the Steinway parlor grand to Lisetta when the family moved to Norfolk.) The girls' practice time affected the whole household. Walter had to read the evening newspaper with a difficult Czerny study in the background; Lisetta could not call upon the girls to help her with supper or to do the dishes; Marleen had to finish her own piano practice before her sisters got home from high school.

In November, Lisetta drove the girls to Omaha to shop for gowns for the recital. Jeannine chose a light green satin gown and Fauneil a cherry red gown in the same style. They felt that the gowns and the green plants and poinsettias on the stage would be perfect at Christmas-time.

The Getzmer household was also involved in advertising the recital in Norfolk and Hoskins. Walter had posters and flyers printed; he handed out the flyers to his real estate clients, business associates, and farm tenants. Jeannine and Fauneil put up posters at school and in various stores. Lisetta planned a reception at the house and sent out invitations to friends and relatives. Marleen was encouraged to help in preparing the food for the reception.

       *   *   *

At 7:45 p.m. on December 3rd, 1950, Walter, Lisetta, and Marleen were ushered to their seats in the auditorium. They studied the program as they waited for the performance to begin. "Here we go," whispered Lisetta to Marleen as the lights dimmed.

Program

Chaconne in D Minor   J.S. Bach/Busoni
Etude Op. 10 No. 5   Frederic Chopin
          Miss Fauneil Getzmer, Pianist

Rhapsodie Op. 119 No. 4   Johannes Brahms
Etude Op. 25 No. 9   Frederic Chopin
          Miss Jeannine Getzmer, Pianist

Symphonic Etude Op. 13 No. 12   Robert Schumann
Concert Etude Op. 36   Edward MacDowell
          Miss Theresa Wilson, Pianist

Sogno D'Amore   Vincenzo De Crescenzo
The Blue Danube   .Johann Strauss
          Miss Jeannine Getzmer, Soprano
          Miss Fauneil Getzmer, Accompanist

Concerto No. 3 in C Ludwig van Beethoven Rondo
          Miss Theresa Wilson, Soloist
          Miss Jane Hillman, Second Piano

Concerto No. 1 in E-flat   Franz Liszt Allegro
      Quasi Adagio
          Miss Jeannine Getzmer, Soloist
          Miss Fauneil Getzmer, Second Piano
    Allegretto Vivace
    Allegro Marziale Animato
          Miss Fauneil Getzmer, Soloist
          Miss Jeannine Getzmer, Second Piano

Presentation of Diplomas Reverend Francis E. Kubart

The following day, <u>The Norfolk Daily News</u> reported that "between six and seven hundred persons left enthusiastic applause ringing in the ears of three talented pianists," that "each one clearly demonstrated she had spent many hours practicing," that "Jeannine delighted her audience with her vocal selections," that "Miss Wilson played with fine effect and interpretation," and that "the Getzmer sisters charmed the audience with an excellent presentation of a difficult concerto."

For weeks after the recital, Walter heard comments from friends, relatives, and clients.

"Walt, I saw the picture of your girls in the paper," said Fred Thomas.

"Ja, that was quite a concert," answered Walter proudly.

"Tell me, Walt, do you really like all that high-falutin' music?"

"Sure. Sure do, especially when my girls are making it."

*   *   *

Part III
Letting Go

Chapter XII
College Days

In the fall of 1951, Jeannine started college at Wayne State Teacher's College in Wayne, Nebraska. Fauneil began her senior year at Norfolk High School. During the summer, Walter had purchased an old secondhand Chevy coupe for the girls. Fauneil drove this to and from school and to Wayne to pick up Jeannine from college so that she could come home on the weekends.

Fauneil, at "sweet 16," began dating Roger, who became her first love. They became inseparable and independent of rules set by their elders; they held hands at school, broke curfews, and played hooky one day from school. Roger met Fauneil at school, and instead of going inside, they drove his little, old Morris to Madison, where they spent the day "bumming around."

They returned home at the end of the school day. What a surprise Fauneil had when she entered the house! Both mothers were in the living room. The school attendance clerk had become suspicious and had called their homes. Roger and Fauneil were given the punishment of separation from each other for thirty days. However, they still had the summer together – putt, putting around in Roger's motor scooter, swimming, playing tennis, square-dancing, watching movies at the drive-in, and going for rides in the country.

At the end of the summer, Fauneil wanted to use her Regents' scholarship to the University of Nebraska, and Jeannine wanted to transfer there from Wayne. Walter was against it. He had just taken on a mortgage for a third farm and was worried about expenses at the "U". Norfolk Junior College was almost free, and Wayne State was inexpensive. The girls had two sensible, inexpensive choices. Lisetta stepped in to support the girls. "Walt, Fauneil was first in her class. She has earned the right to go to the "U". As a music major, she deserves the good music training she will get there."

"But Jeannine is already at Wayne State. She doesn't need to go to the "U" because Fauneil is."

"Remember Jeannine's illness as a sophomore, how she struggled through it and went on to become a beautiful singer and pianist. Have you forgotten that recital, Walt?" Walter was silent, unable to respond with a fair argument.

"You're right, Lisetta," he finally said. "I'll manage the money somehow."

*   *   *

The last week of August, Walter and Lisetta drove the girls to Lincoln for Rush Week at the "U". Lisetta liked the idea of their joining a sorority where they would be supervised by the housemother. They took along all of the girls' school clothes: skirts, sweaters, blouses, saddle shoes, and penny loafers for the classroom; dresses and high-heeled pumps for dresswear; trousers and tennis shoes for casual wear;

jackets for fall; heavy coats, woolen scarves, mittens, and rubber boots for winter.

"Now remember to follow the dress code when you go to class," said Lisetta. "No trousers in the classroom."

"Write," ordered Walter, "and come home sometimes on the weekends."

As they pulled away, Lisetta said, "The house is going to seem empty without the girls."

"We still have Marleen at home," answered Walter.

"Do you know, Walt, that there are over eight thousand students at the "U"? That's only four thousand less than we have in the whole town of Norfolk."

"Ja. They're going to feel lost there. I'll bet they'll be coming home almost every weekend," surmised Walter.

*   *   *

When October turned into November, and the girls had still not come home for a weekend visit, Walter complained to Lisetta, "They can't have that much homework on the weekends."

"It's not just homework, Walt. There are social functions at the sorority on the weekends."

"Well, they're coming home for Thanksgiving, aren't they?"

*   *   *

As fall turned into winter, Walter continued to sorely miss the girls. *If only they had gone to Norfolk Junior College*, he thought, *they would still be at home, and it would be cheaper.* He wished that his stomach would stop burning. Dr. Brauer had diagnosed a duodenal ulcer, which was crusting over and gradually closing the opening to his small intestines.

Lisetta was having a hard time, too. One afternoon, she took the car and drove out to see Minnie. As Lisetta pulled into the yard, Minnie was just coming out of the hen house with a basket of eggs. "Come into the kitchen, Zettie," she said. "I got a chocolate cake, and I'll put on a pot of coffee." Lisetta followed Minnie into the house and down the basement stairs.

"Are you still living down here, Ma?"

"Just for meals. I like it down here because it's cool, and I can slop around. That way my upstairs kitchen always looks good if I happen to get a visitor."

"I came to visit, and here we are in the basement."

"Ach, Zettie, you're no visitor."

"I haven't seen much of you lately, Ma. You're really becoming quite a hermit."

"I have my visitors. Little Loy comes over from Lyle's. He tells me about school, and I make taffy for him."

"I'm worried about your being alone here at night, Ma."

"I can take care of myself, Zettie. I keep a small pistol by my bed."

"I didn't know that. Have you ever needed it?"

"Just once. A man in a cowboy hat came into the yard one afternoon and asked me a lot of questions. About two o'clock in the morning, the dog started barking. I turned on the yard light, and there he was, standing and looking at the house. *Der Verruckte* still had his cowboy hat on! I opened the window and yelled, 'Get off my land!' Then I shot my pistol three times in the air. He high-tailed it out of here." Lisetta shook her head. "That just shows how dangerous it is for you to be alone out here."

"Ach, Zettie, I can take care of myself."

Lisetta changed the subject. "Walt is in the hospital again with his duodenal ulcer."

"He worries too much."

"He misses the girls, too. We both do. Ma, when Dad died, how did you manage to keep up your spirits?"

"Work, Zettie. I kept busy, and I had to learn how to manage things. I found I liked being the boss."

"You still do, Ma." Minnie smiled and nodded.

"You know, Ma, I feel like I've lost a part of myself."

"You have, Zettie, but you have to try for happiness inside." She pointed to her heart. "You can't depend on someone else for it, not even in your own family."

As Lisetta was leaving, Minnie handed her a check for four thousand dollars. Surprised, Lisetta asked, "What's *this*, Ma?"

"Our talk reminded me. In Gus's will, this farm, the forty acres, and four thousand dollars were to someday be yours. Then the depression came along. The land and house will be yours when I die, but I want you to have the cash now."

"Thank you, Ma. I wish Dad were here so I could thank him, too."

"Use it for yourself, Zettie. Get something you've always wanted."

*   *   *

On the way home, Lisetta thought about Minnie's words: "You have to try for happiness inside." *Easier said than done*, thought Lisetta. *Some women fill up their days with social activities or sports; some take on careers; none of that appeals to me.*

However, there was one thing that Lisetta had always wanted – to complete her bachelor's degree. From Minnie she had the money now, and she had the time to study. She could commute to Wayne State. But she wondered if Walt could handle it. Before discussing it with him, she decided to get some information from Wayne State. She wrote to the Admissions Office, asking them to review her transcripts and to send her a list of requirements needed to complete her degree.

She received a disappointing response.   Many of the courses she had taken years ago would need to be repeated because of changes in the curriculum. She estimated that it would take her three years instead of two to complete her degree. She wasn't sure that she wanted to devote three years of her life to school. Besides, she decided, Walt didn't need the pressure of three "girls" in college at the same time.

*   *   *

While Walter and Lisetta were missing their daughters at 1208 Nebraska Avenue, Jeannine and Fauneil were happy at Alpha Xi Delta, located at 1619 "R" Street in Lincoln. The girls thought that "their" house was the loveliest on campus. Most of the other houses were built of brick whereas the Alpha Xi house was made of beige-colored stone from the Nebraska Sandhills. It was a three-story house with a partial fourth story, which was used as the chapter room, and a basement, which contained a large dining room for evening meals. At the front of the house were two patios, the lower one covered, the upper one open. The upper patio was used mainly for the coeds to listen to an unexpected serenade from fraternity boys.

The lower floor contained a living room large enough for the entire chapter. A parlor grand piano, mainly played by Fauneil, took up one corner of the room. Two smaller rooms led off the living room, one a tea room, the other a television room. To the left of the entrance hall, was an elegant sitting room with full-length Romanesque-style windows. Archways on the lower floor repeated the Romanesque feature.

In the second and third stories, the bedrooms were located, with each bedroom occupied by two or three girls. In addition, there were a lounge area, a library, and a big tiled bathroom with plenty of showers, sinks, and toilets. For privacy, one telephone was located at the end of a narrow hall on each floor. (One of the pledge duties was to answer the phone and then summon the active being called.)

The personnel managing the house were the house mother, who had her own quarters, the maids, and the busboys who served the Alpha Xi*s* at dinnertime.

In contrast to their new "home," Jeannine and Fauneil had been accustomed to living in humble houses, two which lacked indoor plumbing. When the family moved to Minnie's house in Norfolk, they *luxuriated* in a small bathroom with one toilet, one sink, and a bathtub without an overhead shower.

On the first floor, there were a living room, dining room, kitchen, and two bedrooms with small walk-in closets. The basement was mainly for utilities: rooms used for laundry, food storage, tools and a furnace.

By the time Jeannine and Fauneil were in high school, Walter and Lisetta had converted the attic into living quarters: a hall with bookshelves, a luggage/storage room, a small half bath, and a long, large bedroom which contained a single bed and nightstand for each girl, several dressers, a dressing table, a desk, and an entertainment center with two chairs and a phonograph. (It was organized similarly to the Feiler house they had wanted to purchase in Hoskins.)

Because the attic was low and had room for small windows only on the west and the east sides, a good crosswind for nighttime sleeping was non-existent. The common complaint in the summertime was, "It's like an oven upstairs."

After Jeannine and Fauneil moved into the Alpha Xi Delta house, they felt as though they were living in a mansion. Although they missed their parents and their sister, they were reluctant to leave the luxury of the mansion, their new friends, and the social activities for a return to uncomfortable living quarters.

*   *   *

The year 1954 marked the centennial of Nebraska's existence as a territory. Throughout the 1953-1954 school year, the University observed the centennial. The Cornhusker Yearbook included a dedication page to the pioneers with the statement, "The spirit of a people is in its history." The campus newspaper, "The Nebraskan," included historical articles about the university's humble beginnings: (Cows had grazed on campus when the "U" first opened its doors on September 7, 1871. At first the "U" consisted only of a single College of Literature for eight regular students, including one woman, and twelve irregular students and of a preparatory Latin school of 110 pupils.)

Throughout the school year, there were pageants, parades, displays, dances (called "hops"), and a skit at the Coed Follies, featuring a pioneer theme. In the spring, Walter and Lisetta drove to Lincoln to attend a luncheon at Alpha Xi Delta, where parents were honored and then entertained with a pioneer theme enacted in a "little brown jug" skit.

* * *

For Jeannine and Fauneil, the major social event of the year was the annual dinner-dance in May. It was held in the ballroom of the Cornhusker Hotel. The Alpha Xis had decorated the tables with "pioneer" decorations, but the occasion was a formal one.

Each coed tried to look her best for the evening in a beautiful gown and coiffed hair and manicured nails. With having to keep her nails short for piano playing, Fauneil had only one solution for her short nails – to wear a set of false nails. After dressing for the evening, Fauneil cut false nails to fit her fingers, adhered them with nail cement, cut them to shape, and applied Spanish Rose nail polish, a color that complimented her blue tulle gown.

At the dinner-dance, all went well at first. Fauneil showed off her long, beautiful nails as she handled her utensils and napkin at the dinner. After dinner, she strolled to the table where Jeannine was seated. "Warm, isn't it?" she asked Jeannine, fanning herself. Jeannine had a puzzled look on her face.

Fauneil excused herself and headed for the restroom. In the stall, she had no trouble rolling down her rubber girdle (the popular choice of girdles for female coeds in 1954), but pulling it up again became a calamity. The girdle stuck to her skin, and she could only tug at it with her fingers in a flat position. Tug after tug, the girdle refused to budge. With time running short, she tugged hard with both fingers and nails; all but two of her false nails pulled off, leaving white splotches of cement on her natural nails.

Returning to the table, she tucked her hands under her armpits. "Line up for the bunny hop!" shouted the band leader. Fauneil's date pulled her up to join the line; her hands were now fully visible. "What happened to your nails?" her date asked as the music ended and he seated her at their table.

"It's a tale best untold," answered Fauneil, trying for a literary retort.

* * *

When summer vacation began, the girls returned to Norfolk. Walter encouraged them to get summer jobs to help pay for new clothes they would want for the next year. Jeannine found a job baby-sitting for a neighbor, and Fauneil was hired as an evening cashier at the Rialto Theater. On the occasions when the family sat down to eat together, there was sometimes a lack of harmony. When Jeannine complained about the heat in the girls' upstairs bedroom, Walter took her complaints as a lack of gratitude. When Fauneil tried to converse about information from her psychology class, Walter called her a "know-it-all." Only 13-year-old Marleen could please him.

"Walt," said Lisetta after a family discord at the dinner table, "You're so touchy and irritable. Don't you realize that Jeannine and Fauneil are becoming young adults and can't be treated like children anymore?"

"I'm sorry, Lisetta. I'm feeling so miserable most of the time with this burning sensation in my stomach, and I'm tired of vomiting after every meal."

"Dr. Brauer has put you on a bland diet. I'm trying not to use spices, and you need to drink more milk."

"I'm tired of milk. Tired, tired, tired of milk and of worrying about money."

"Jeannine and Fauneil are home now. You have three months before the bills start again, so take the summer to enjoy some relaxation. Go fishing! You love that."

Walter sat down for his evening reading. Unfortunately, the article was about the **cost** of World War II and the destruction which the war had caused.

*   *   *

War News
The Aftermath of World War II

World War II was the most costly and destructive of any war in history. The price of the war to the U.S. was $341,000,000,000. The price to Germany was $272,000,000,000. Axis powers had monetary redresses to make: In 1952, West Germany was ordered to pay more

106

than three billion marks to Israel for victims of the holocaust who were now without family.

Rebuilding in cities that had been bombed was a tremendous undertaking. By 1950, the "rubble women" of West Germany had finally cleared away the rubble, and the rebuilding had begun. Dresden had been completely razed, but the Germans had determined to rebuild it in its Baroque splendor, a huge but possible undertaking because the architectural plans for the original buildings had been saved. The Allies, too, lost magnificent structures and treasures. In England, many beautiful cathedrals and churches were destroyed. Russia lost majestic palaces and irreplaceable works of art.

   No country affected by the war was without a severe aftermath.

*   *   *

Chapter XIII
Walter's Illness

In early October, Lisetta invited guests to celebrate their 22nd wedding anniversary. It was a small dinner party with her brother, Lyle, and his wife Marcella and her cousin, Loretta, and her husband Oliver. During the meal, they first discussed family and local news.

"What do you hear from Hank in California?" asked Lyle.

"Hank and Tillie are having a hard time," answered Walter. "They lost Howard, their second son, in the war in Korea," added Lisetta.

"In combat?" asked Lyle.

"Ja. They're not sure how."

"That whole war has been a mess," said Lyle, "dragging on for three years." Oliver joined in. "President Truman should have let General MacArthur pursue the communists when we already had the North Koreans in control."

"Truman was trying to prevent a showdown between the U.S. and the U.S.S.R.," countered Lyle.

"Eisenhower kept his promise," said Loretta. "He promised to end the war if he was elected, and he did."

"But the problems remain," added Lisetta. "The United Nation's goal was to unite North and South Korea, but the U.S. left the 38th parallel in place and a divided Korea."

"Think of the lives lost, just to hold the line," remarked Oliver, who was good at remembering figures. "Thirty-four thousand Americans, seventy thousand South Koreans, and two million North Koreans and Chinese."

"I didn't realize that the toll was so high," commented Marcella.

Oliver became reflective. "All six of us at this table have already experienced three wars in our lifetime, and this won't be the last."

"You're right," agreed Lisetta. "As the *Bible* says, *there will be wars and rumors of wars until the end of the world.*"

Walter excused himself and hurried to the bathroom. Through the closed door, everyone could hear him retching.

"I guess our conversation upset Walt," said Oliver to Lisetta.

"No, it's his ulcers. They're getting worse all the time."

*   *   *

War News – Korea
June 1950 – July 1953

The Korean conflict began in the Great Depression of the 1930s, when extremes of right and left political groups formed. Two Koreas began to emerge in 1931 when Japan became an imperial aggressor against northeast China (Manchuria), which the North Koreans called "Greater Korea."

Korea had become a protectorate of Japan in 1905 and a colony in 1910. Most Koreans saw this imperial rule as humiliating. In 1945, at the end of World War II, North Korea remained anti-Japan whereas South Korea became essential to Japan's industrial revival.

Civil war broke out in Korea in June 1950 when a border fight occurred, followed by an invasion of the North against troops from the South. The USA, under the leadership of General MacArthur, came to the aid of the South while communist China joined with troops from the North. During the summer of 1950, the South prevailed; during the winter, the North drew MacArthur's troops into the North by receding.

The winter of 1950-1951 was severe, with temperatures dropping to 21 degrees below zero. Americans found themselves unsuccessfully fighting soldiers who were used to the freezing conditions and to guerilla warfare. The North was succeeding, and American soldiers were dying. General MacArthur was removed from command in April of 1951 by President Truman.

Peace negotiations began but were not agreed upon by South Korea. Meanwhile, fighting continued along the 38th *parallel until 1953.   The United Nations declared a demilitarized zone (the DMZ) between the two Koreas. The war became a stalemate, and a divided Korea remained.*

*   *   *

When Jeannine and Fauneil returned to the university in the fall of 1954, Walter's ulcers were getting worse. He felt a bit better by Christmastime, but he had a relapse shortly after. Dr. Brauer advised him to have surgery to remove the acid-producing parts of his stomach.   In spite of his discomfort, Walter kept putting it off. He finally decided to have the surgery in early April at a time when Jeannine and Fauneil were beginning to study for final exams at the university.

*   *   *

Jeannine was in her final year at school. At the sorority, she had been elected treasurer, which added to her workload and responsibility. It was her duty to collect the monthly dues from each of the Alpha Xis, to pay the bills for the house, and to monthly record and balance the debits and credits in the financial ledger. Each Wednesday, she met with Miss Mungy, the very tall, very thin alum in charge of finance.

"Well done, Jeannine," said Miss Mungy as she got up from her chair and headed towards the door. Jeannine watched as Miss Mungy's undies fell from her skinny hips and landed on her shoes. With the grace of an Alpha Xi Delta alum, she bent down, retrieved the undies, put them into her purse, and exited the room. Jeannine was still smiling when a pledge entered and handed her a letter from Walter.

April 11, 1955

Dear Jeannine,

Just a short note before I go to the hospital this morning. It is about 10:00 AM now. By tomorrow at this time, they should have me part way done. Pray for me. I know everything will be okay. Yesterday I deposited $68 to your account. This is the balance on your sewing machine. I put the cost of the machine in addition to what you had for school expenditure.

Well, Jeannine, I must soon be leaving for the hospital, and I'll have to close this short letter. I wish to thank you for being such a considerate girl, and I want you to know that I love you very much. I am proud to have you as my daughter. I have always loved all my daughters very much, and I thank God for the gift of my girls.
Be seeing you in my dreams.

Love,
Daddy

Jeannine felt emotionally touched but disturbed by the letter. She took it to consult with Fauneil. "I don't have a good feeling about this," she confided to Fauneil. "Do you think we should go home?"

"I got a letter from Mom saying the surgery was not life threatening and not to worry," answered Fauneil.

"Okay, we'll just wait until we hear."

* * *

A few days later, Jeannine received a phone call from Lisetta: "Dad isn't doing well. When he started throwing up kernels of stool, Dr. Brauer did exploratory surgery and found that his intestines had crawled through a hole in the peritoneal sac and became strangulated. His condition is critical. He has peritonitis. You and Fauneil had better come right away!"

When the girls stepped into the intensive care ward at the Lutheran Hospital at midnight, they saw their father hooked up to a series of monitors and tubes.

"What are those tubes doing in his abdomen?" Jeannine asked Lisetta.

"Those are for the peritonitis. The nurse pours penicillin through them into the body cavity."

"Is Dad in pain?" asked Fauneil.

"I don't know. He's in and out of consciousness."

"Mom, you look exhausted. Why don't you go home and get some sleep? We'll stay here with Dad tonight," said Jeannine. Fauneil nodded. Lisetta refused to go at first, but by three o'clock, she felt ill from exhaustion. She went home for a few hours of sleep and returned early the next morning. By then, Walter's fever had dropped a few degrees.

"That's a good sign," said Lisetta. "We'll see what Dr. Brauer says when he comes. If he thinks Dad is out of danger now, you girls should return to school."

"Won't you need some help, Mom?" asked Fauneil.

"No. As soon as Dad is moved from intensive care, I'll hire Aunt Lisetta to stay with him around the clock."

* * *

The girls returned to school, and Walter stayed in the hospital a month to recuperate. When he was discharged, he was frail and frazzled; he still had a partial bowel blockage; he had trouble sleeping; his hands shook from nervousness; and he was irrational.

"Lisetta," he insisted one morning, "I need you to go to Doctor Verges and get me something so I can sleep."

"Walt, you know that Dr. Brauer is our doctor."

"Hell, he doesn't care about me! He doesn't even come to see me. Go and get Doctor Verges.! Now!" Lisetta left the house, but she drove to Dr. Brauer's office.

"I'm having trouble with Walt," she confided to Dr. Brauer. "Walt just rants at me, and I don't know what to do for him anymore." Dr. Brauer promised to come by the house when he was through with his hospital visits.

When he stepped into Walter's bedroom that afternoon, Walter turned red with anger. "I told you to get Dr. Verges!" Walter yelled at Lisetta.

"Now, Walt, simmer down," said Dr. Brauer. "You know that Lisetta and I both care about you."

"No, nobody cares about me. And I don't trust **her!**" He pointed his finger at Lisetta.

Lisetta left the room in tears. Dr. Brauer stayed with Walter for several hours, giving him enema after enema until he had worked the bowel blockage loose. On his way out, he handed Lisetta a prescription for sleeping tablets. "I'm sorry for the way he spoke to you, Doctor," said Lisetta.

Doctor Brauer smiled. "He's just off his rocker a bit. He pushed himself so hard for so many years, and now this whole ordeal has been almost more than his constitution can bear. You know, some patients handle severe illness better than others."

After Dr. Brauer had left, Lisetta sat down a moment to rest before getting supper. She reflected upon Walter's irrational behavior and his hurtful remarks to her. As she closed her eyes in tiredness, she thought about Dr. Brauer's comment, *some patients handle severe illness better than others*. Suddenly, she was at her father's bedside in 1928, with a scissors in her hand, ready to cut his nails. *Hello, my Liebchen! Do you think you're old enough to handle a pair of scissors? he said, giving her a smile.*

*   *   *

In May, Lisetta drove Walter to Lincoln for Jeannine's graduation from the University. Since Walter was still too weak and nervous to attend the graduation exercises, Lisetta rented a room for him at the Cornhusker Hotel. Following the ceremony, Lisetta, the girls, and Ralph (Jeannine's fiancé) joined Walter for a celebration in his room.

Jeannine introduced Ralph as her fiancé. "What do you do for a living?" asked Walter.

"I'm a student here at the University, but I've been in the Navy until recently."

"We're planning to marry in August. Then I'll get a teaching job while Ralph finishes college," said Jeannine to Walter.

"I suppose you'll want a big wedding – at **my** expense." Jeannine blushed. "A small one, with Fauneil and Marleen as attendants."

Walter turned to Fauneil. "Are you coming home this summer?" When Fauneil explained that she had a job as a secretary with Harrington Real Estate in Lincoln and that it would begin at the end of May, Walter turned to Ralph and said, "Fauneil doesn't care about me." Ralph responded with a slight shrug. Lisetta pulled Fauneil aside and whispered, "Ignore that. He's still sick. You go ahead with your plans, and let me know if you need anything." Fauneil nodded and avoided Walter's eyes.

*   *   *

Back at home, Walter continued to be difficult, irritable, and convinced that no one cared about him.

"Maybe I shouldn't be planning a formal church wedding," suggested Jeannine to Lisetta.

"Yes, you should! All three of our daughters will get a church wedding," responded Lisetta. Jeannine and Lisetta discussed Walter's moping about the house. "He needs to get back into his business," said Lisetta, "but I can't even get him to drive out to see the farms."

"Maybe we can get him to go fishing," suggested Jeannine. "You know how much he loves to fish."

"Great idea!" Lisetta exclaimed. Later in the day, she called Lyle, who went fishing each summer in Minnesota for northern pike and walleyes. Lyle suggested that the two couples travel to Minnesota together, so that they could encourage Walt to converse again. Lisetta decided to leave Marleen at home with Jeannine, and Lyle and Marcella planned to send their three boys to Minnie's.

*   *   *

For the first few days of their stay at the lake, Walter stubbornly refused to leave the cabin. The first day, he complained that he was too nervous to hold a fishing rod; the second day, that he would get sick in the boat. By the third day, Lyle had had enough of his self-pity.

"Come on, Walt," Lyle ordered. "We're going fishing. Get your rod and your cap! Hurry up! No excuses today."

When they returned at noontime, they were each carrying a string of fish. Lisetta and Marcella could see that Walter was talking away a mile a minute while Lyle nodded his head from time to time.

In the cabin, Lisetta pulled Lyle aside. "It's like a miracle, Lyle. How did you do it?"

"Ach, Zettie, I didn't do a thing. The lake and the fish did it."

*   *   *

Back in Norfolk, Walter began the farm management part of his business, enjoying the sunshine, the fresh air, and the green fields. Gradually he took on his real estate business, and his recovery was well on its way.

*   *   *

Chapter XIV
Fauneil

In Lincoln, Fauneil was coping with living in the attic of a three-story house. It was hot when she climbed the stairs to her apartment, she immediately jumped into a tub of cool water and soaked until her body had heated the water. When she wrote to Lisetta about her living conditions, Lisetta drove to Lincoln with a fan, a load of towels, and some old tableware and cooking utensils.

On the weekends, Fauneil escaped to a nearby public swimming pool. One Saturday, she saw a tall, slim, beautifully tanned young man, who was the best-looking guy she had seen since Roger. She watched him throughout the afternoon as he dived and swam. However, he didn't appear to notice her.

Midway in the week, Fauneil was on her way to shop on "O" Street during her lunch break when she bumped into "the golden boy." He stopped and said, "It's you! I saw you at the swimming pool on Saturday."

"I saw you, too," answered Fauneil.

"That perfume you're wearing – is that *Arpege?*"

"Good guess. Do you like it?" That was the beginning of a short, romantic relationship between a sailor on leave and a college student on summer break.

When Leroy left Lincoln to return to his naval base in San Diego, Fauneil drove to Norfolk for Jeannine's wedding. While there, she confided to Lisetta about her romance with Leroy.

"I think he's the one for me, Mom." Lisetta smiled. "You're young yet. Give it time."

*   *   *

The fall semester of 1955 began Fauneil's senior year at the "U". It was a very busy one: classes in the mornings, Harrington's in the afternoons, and studying in the evenings. Her morning classes included one she taught as a student teacher – junior high English in the fall semester, senior high English in the spring semester. Her supervisor sent numerous education majors to watch Fauneil perform in the classroom as she exhibited both vivacity and control of her students. Because of all of her musical "on-stage" experiences, she was inspired rather than nervous by an audience.

Mary, the secretary in the supervisor's office, had been Fauneil's high school friend and her freshman roommate at the "U". Through conversations, Mary and Fauneil found that they had a shared interest in the naval base at San Diego. Mary's husband and Fauneil's boyfriend were both stationed there. Mary planned to spend Christmas vacation in San Diego, and Fauneil and Leroy had discussed her joining him there. *What a coincidence,* thought Fauneil. *I can afford my own plane ticket, so I don't need to ask Dad for money.* However, when she wrote home about her plans, Walter forbade her to go to San Diego, saying that her place was at home at Christmastime. Besides, he reminded her, he was still paying the majority of her expenses at the "U".

When Fauneil wrote the news to Leroy, he did not seem upset. Instead, he promised to call her on New Year's Day, when they would make another plan.

*   *   *

New Year's Day came and went. No phone call from Leroy. As the weeks went by, there were no letters from him. Fauneil began her final semester at the University with a heavy heart. She was extremely busy and tried not to think about Leroy, but walking to and from Harrington's each day gave her time to contemplate.

In the spring, Fauneil's attention turned to the future. She had interviews with scouts from Nebraska, Kansas, Mississippi, and Arizona for a teaching position in the fall. One day near the end of the school year, she received a letter from Leroy. Her hands were shaking as she opened the envelope. In his brief letter, he apologized for not calling on New Year's Day. He had married a girl in San Diego. The marriage had foundered. Their divorce was finalized. "I still love you," he had added. "Can you forgive me?"

Fauneil sat down for a minute and reflected on the humiliation and depression she had endured during her last semester. She got up, tore the letter in two, and tossed it into the wastebasket. Her feeling towards Leroy was one of disgust. She thought of Walter's refusal to let her go and was now grateful for his firmness. He had saved her from making one of the biggest mistakes of her lifetime.

Shortly before the end of school, Eileen, a sorority sister, told Fauneil about a summer study tour of Europe with the University of South Dakota for six units of college credit. Eileen's parents were giving her the trip as a graduation present, and she wondered if Fauneil would consider joining her. Fauneil knew that Walter would not give her the money; however, he might loan it to her. When she discussed it with Lisetta and Walter, he was against her going so far away from home and then starting her teaching career with $1,500 of debt. Fauneil explained the details of the trip as though he had agreed to it:

The trip would last from late May until late August, and all expenses would be covered with the $1,500. The journey would start by train to Montreal, where the travelers would board an ocean liner, taking them via the St. Lawrence River to the Atlantic Ocean and across to England. In Europe, they would visit eleven countries, with an emphasis on England, France, Germany, and Italy. Two language professors from the University of South Dakota would be their chaperones and guides. Dr. Hartman, a native German, spoke German, Norwegian, Swedish, and Danish; his wife spoke French, Italian, and Spanish. At the end of the summer tour, each student seeking six units of graduate credit would have the time to write a paper on the return trip across the Atlantic, from Le Havre, France to New York City. The final leg of the journey would be via train back to South Dakota.

"Mom and Dad, if I get the teaching position in Arizona, the Tucson Public Schools requires a bachelor's degree plus six units of graduate credit for a beginning teacher. I would have to go to summer school somewhere – why not to Europe?"

Lisetta was the first to speak. "This would be ideal for you, Fauneil, with your interests in literature and music."

Fauneil smiled and turned to Walter. "Dad, you saved me from what would have been one of the **worst** mistakes of my life – going to San Diego to see a sailor. If I had gotten tied up with him, I would have missed one of the **best** opportunities of my lifetime – this study tour of Europe."

Walter was happy to be appreciated by his middle daughter, the independent one. "Well," he said, "I won't lend you the money, but if you can get a loan from the bank, I'll co-sign it."

"Thanks, Dad. School districts in four different states are interested in me; I'm sure that the bank won't turn me down for a loan."

Walter insisted on some control of Fauneil's venture:
"Fauneil, you will need to repay the loan in 12   months; I expect you to write letters to the family throughout the trip; you may take my Bell and Howell movie camera with you so you can send us pictures along the way, and I want you to buy yourself a diary so you can make daily entries throughout the trip. We will want you to share the diary with us when you return, so be careful what you write."

"Yes, Dad. Any requests, Mom?" Lisetta smiled. "I think you have enough from Dad."

Fauneil bought herself a little red leather diary in which she could enter the date, the itinerary, and notes of the highlights of each day. Her notes, she felt, would be helpful in fulfilling her letter-writing promise and later when she needed to write her academic paper on the way to New York City from Le Havre, France.

*   *   *

Fauneil graduated *in absentia* from the University of Nebraska because the study tour began earlier. She packed her belongings into her car, waved goodbye to Alpha Xi Delta, and headed for Norfolk. She only had a day to get ready for her trip.

Walter and Lisetta drove Fauneil to Yankton, South Dakota to board the train to Chicago, where she would change for one headed to Montreal. On the way, they discussed Europe, especially Germany.

"It's only been eleven years since World War II ended," said Walter.

"Ja, Walt," agreed Lisetta. "Your Uncle Richard's family are in Eastern Berlin, under the control of the U.S.S.R now."

"That whole section of Berlin is off limits to Americans, so you couldn't visit them if you wanted to," said Walter to Fauneil.

"I know," she answered. "East Berlin is not in our itinerary. The communists are even preventing East Berliners from visiting relatives in West Berlin."

"Make sure you take pictures of destruction from bombing during the war," advised Walter.

"And if you see people living in poverty, be kind. You'll seem like a rich American to them," added Lisetta.

"I'll be careful not to come across as *the ugly American*," promised Fauneil.

* * *

Fauneil was silent for a while, reflecting on information about the war from her history class. The cost of money and lives had been appalling.

War News, the Aftermath of World War II

Military Deaths (between 1937 and 1945)		Civilian Deaths	
USSR	10,700,000	China	16,200,000
Germany	5,533,000	USSR	12,400,000
China	3,800,000	Others	8,450,000
Japan	2,120,000	Poland	5,440,000
Others	1,422,500	Germany	1,760,000
Britain and the Commonwealth	575,000	Britain and the Commonwealth	1,568,500
USA	416,800	Japan	1,000,000
Italy	301,400	France	350,000
France	217,600	Italy	153,100
Poland	160,000	USA	0

Notes:

The loss of lives was unequally spread. Poland lost 16% of its population; the USA lost 1/3 of 1% of its population.

1. *Four times as many Allied citizens died as Axis ones.*
2. *The Nazis' murderous policy towards Soviet civilians caused 12,000,000 deaths.*
3. *Hitler's policy of exterminating all Jews caused 16,000,000 Jewish deaths, 40% of the world's Jewish population.*
4. *More civilians died than soldiers in the war.*
5. *Modern estimates of the total death toll for World War II are from 55,000,000 to over 70,000,000 people.*

*   *   *   *

Chapter XV
Letters from Fauneil

Letter to Minnie   June 21, 1956

> *Dear Grandma,*
>
> *Our ship has arrived, and I am writing on the bus from Southampton, a seaport, to London in England. The countryside, with rolling green pastures, reminds me of Nebraska in the spring. Instead of fences dividing the fields, the farmers plant tall bush hedges between properties. Their houses are made of brick or stone and topped with chimneys which look like spools of thread. They remind me of your threading your embroidery needles while we visited during summer vacation from school.*
>
> *Love, Fauneil*

*   *   *

Letter to Walter and Lisetta   June 21, 1956

> *Dear Mom and Dad,*
>
> *I am writing from London. Our train trip from Southampton to London was beautiful – the countryside so green and the farmers' cottages so quaint. Upon arriving in London, we toured the city from the upper deck of a sightseeing bus. In case of rain (always likely here), we carried our umbrellas.*

Our tour included Westminster Abbey, across from the Houses of Parliament, made of carved stone and in the Gothic style. Next was the Tower of London with its deep ravine, which was once a moat. The Tower is actually a series of buildings: a castle built by William the Conqueror in the 11th century; the "Bloody Tower," where the two little princes were murdered by orders from Richard III; and a building housing the crown jewels. We left the bus for this part of the tour, and when we were leaving two hours later, the bus took us across the Tower Bridge, crossing the Thames River.

London is so full of history, we would have to stay here all summer to see everything.

Love, Fauneil

*   *   *

Letter to Jeannine   June 22, 1956

Dear Jeannine,

Today was a glorious day of art and music! John, an art student and a member of our tour group, and I spent the day at the Tate Galleries. I was fortunate to be with him because he enjoyed sharing his knowledge of art with me.

My favorite English painters were Reynolds, Gainsborough, and Turner. We also saw many paintings of the French Impressionists, and John explained the techniques of each.
My favorites of these were Monet and Renoir.

After dinner, our tour attended a performance of the opera, "La Boheme," at Sadler's Wells. I cried when I heard the soprano diva sing some of the arias which I accompanied on the piano when you practiced them. Thank God for music that speaks to the soul!

Love, Fauneil

*   *   *

Letter to Mary   June 23, 1956

Dear Mary,

A very eventful day! A bus drove us from our London Hotel to Windsor, where the streets were lined with people waiting to catch glimpses of Queen Elizabeth. The castle was guarded by soldiers in red uniforms and tall black hats. Our next stop was Oxford. On foot we toured Christ College at Oxford University, the Oxford Cathedral with its lovely rose stained-glass window, and the round-shaped Bodleian Library, which houses the largest collection of books in the world.

After lunch, the bus drove us to "Shakespeare Land." We had a walking tour here of Shakespeare's home, Anne Hathaway's charming hatched cottage (the ceilings were so low, the taller guys had to bend down while walking through the cottage), and the Memorial Theater, where we attended "Othello" in the evening. As we strolled back to the bus, we all agreed that the superior acting, scenery, and lighting had brought the play alive.

A beautiful moon shining upon the Avon River led us back to the bus. I thought of you, Mary, with all of your acting roles at Norfolk High School and of the Shakespeare class we took at the "U." Cheerio!

Love, Fauneil

*   *   *

Letter to Lisetta and Walter   June 24, 1956

Dear Mom and Dad,

We spent the morning with "pomp and circumstance," viewing from the outside the gardens and the London residence of the royal family – Buckingham Palace. Like the many tourists and Englishmen standing outside of the wrought-iron gates and fences, we watched the Horse Guards ride through the gates. The horses were groomed to perfection. (Grandpa Bech would have been jealous). The riders in their bright uniforms looked very snooty as they passed by, with noses in the air, expressionless faces, and eyes ignoring the crowd.

What a contrast we experienced in the afternoon: a visit to Petticoat Lane in the slum section of London. Mobs of people were buying, selling, or bartering their wares set out on tables or push-carts. Entire blocks in this section contained only rubble from the bombs that had destroyed the buildings and many Londoners who had not made it in time to the underground shelters during World War II. As you know, Hitler had determined to completely destroy London in order to bring Britain to its knees. (I can only imagine what the war years had been like for the British). As we took the double-decker bus back to the hotel, I was thinking about the contrast today – the English had repaired first their palaces, cathedrals, and fashionable sections of the city, and had largely left this section of the city to fend for itself.

I am enjoying my trip and learning so much. Today was a truly historical day for me. It gave me an understanding of the consequences of World War II that I had not had as an American.
Love, Fauneil

* * *

Letter to Minnie   June 28 & 29, 1956

Dear Grandma,

We traveled by train all day in Norway, headed for Oslo, the capitol. The train was packed with many children who were going to an athletic event in Oslo – not a restful ride with all of the noise they were making.

The next morning in Oslo, we visited Vigiland Park, where we studied sculptures depicting the cycle of life: birth, childhood, adulthood, and death. Our next stop was the

Lutheran Cathedral, which was very large, but its architecture was too modern for my taste.

After lunch, we took a bus to Bighoey Peninsula, where we saw ships of the ancient Vikings. They were made of wood, which had rotted, but some were well enough preserved to give us a sense of what it was like to sail the North Sea to England, Iceland, Denmark, etc.

Our last stop was to see the cottages from the 1500's, which had sod roofs planted with grass and flowers. I thought of the stories you told us about your pioneer mother living on the prairie – to me, Great Grandmother Augusta.

Love, Fauneil

*   *   *

Letter to Mary   July 6 & 7, 1956

Dear Mary,

In the morning, we arrived in Essen in the Ruhr district of Germany. A visit of the Sieman's Factory, which manufactures steam and electrical equipment, included a stop in the workers' canteen. Driving past very drab gray or tan, boxy-looking stucco houses, we headed for Cologne. The Gothic Cathedral, with its gorgeous stained-glass windows was a welcome change from Essen.

Our destination for dinner was the Stern Hotel in Bonn, the capitol of Germany. At dinner, I sat next to Sanna Lohre, an older member of our group, and her son John, who is stationed In Essen.

*He is a lieutenant in the army and is working there
as an industrial engineer to help rebuild Germany
from World War II destruction. He is intelligent and
good-looking and plans to see more of his mother
while she is in Germany. Hmm*

Love, Fauneil

*   *   *

Letter to Marleen   July 8 & 9, 1956

Dear Marleen,

*Our inn here at Bonn overlooks the Rhine
River, on which we took a boat trip. The
passengers were drinking Mosel and Rhine wine,
which we all thought delicious. However, the ox
tongue was not to our liking. The scenery along the
Rhine was spectacular: vineyards on the hillsides,
old castles, and the famous Rock of Lorelei.*

*The next day we took a boat cruise to
Rudesheim, which is known for its Rhine wine and
its folk music festivals. (Our outing on the river
recalled to me our annual fishing trip to northern
Minnesota with Dad.) In the evening, upon
returning to our inn, Eileen and I found a box of
"sweeties" in our room. The next morning, we
learned that a young South African had found his
way into our room, hoping to strike up an
acquaintance. We ignored him at breakfast time,
and our group was soon on its way to our next
destination.*

Love, Fauneil

Letter to Mary   July 10 & 11, 1956

Dear Mary,

Our morning was spent in visiting Heidelberg University and in taking the funicular up the mountain to a ruined castle. In the cellar of the castle, we saw the biggest wine barrel in the world, guarded by Perkes, the dwarf.

The evening was exciting. Lieutenant John Lohre had come to Heidelberg to see his mother, Sanna. The three of us had inner together. John and I were attracted to each other, so we went night-clubbing after dinner, first to Cave 57, a hangout for the students at Heidelberg and then to the Red Ox, where we sampled Mosel wine and talked, getting acquainted. By 2:00 P.M., we felt as though we had known each other for years and were sorry to see the evening end. John had to get back to base and couldn't accompany us the next day to Rothenburg, a picturesque town dating back to medieval days.

Auf Wiedersehen! Fauneil

* * *

Letter to Mary   July 13 & 14, 1956

Dear Mary,

In the morning in Munich, we visited the station for Radio Free Europe. Our host was Art Linkletter's son, who explained how the station manages to broadcast to communist satellite countries.

For lunch we went to the Hofbrauhaus and joined Germans at long wooden tables for Bier, Brot und Wurst. In the afternoon, we attended a concert of vocal and instrumental numbers from the 13th through the 16th centuries, using the instruments of those times. What a treat!

When we returned to our hotel, John Lohre was there – he had managed to get another short leave. We went to a small, intimate night club with a good orchestra and a ceiling of glass with colored moving lights. Very romantic! We drank wine, danced, and talked until 3:00 A.M.

John had to return to the base the next day and couldn't accompany us to Herrenchiemsee Island, where we toured a castle built by Ludwig II, who was called "Crazy Ludwig of Bavaria." Before drowning himself at thirty, he had impoverished the peasants to build this castle to rival that of Louis XIV at Versailles. Bavaria has certainly been a romantic and interesting historic place.

Auf Wiedersehen, Fauneil

* * *

Letter to Lisetta and Walter   July 16, 17, & 18, 1956

Dear Mom and Dad,

Leaving Germany behind, we drove all day through the spectacular high Alps to Salzburg, Austria. In the evening, we went to the Puppet

Theater, where the Marionetten performed Tchaikovsky's "Nutcracker Suite."

We left Austria early the next morning to cross back over into Germany, to Berchtesgaden, Hitler's favorite hideout during the war. Then we drove back into the Alps to the charming village of Heiligenblut, which is situated in a valley with the Grossglockner (13,785 ft.) in the distance. From there, we continued through the Alps into the Dolomite Mountains in Italy. These seemed barren and low in comparison to the Alps.

As we neared Venice, the terrain became Mediterranean, with palm and magnolia trees and white stucco houses with red-tiled roofs. Entering Venice, we changed to a motorboat for cruising the green, stagnant waterways (canals), passing gondoliers wearing black trousers, white shirts, red sashes, and wide-brimmed hats. The gondolas were low enough to pass under the many bridges over the canals, which were built so that pedestrians can cross on foot or by bicycle.

Our destination was Lido Island, where we can swim tomorrow in the Adriatic Ocean. The scenery today was so unlike that of Nebraska, I felt like a tourist – which I am!

Love, Fauneil

*   *   *

Letter to Jeannine   July 24, 1956

Dear Jeannine,

We went sightseeing all day in Rome, first by bus past the Monument of Victor Emmanuel II, who brought about the unification of Italy; then the Campidoglio with its many steps; the Pantheon, a circular building erected in 727 B.C. We stretched our legs when we walked to the Trevi Fountain, where we all tossed coins over our shoulders into the fountain.

In the afternoon, we visited the Vatican, built by Emperor Constantine. The architecture of the building is Gothic, but the decoration inside is Baroque. The cathedral was built to symbolize the body of Christ: the dome is the head; the two rows of colonnades are his outstretched arms. Inside the cathedral is a very touching statue by Michelangelo of Mary holding the crucified body of Christ. I stared at it a long time with tears in my eyes and a lump in my throat.

Next, we toured the Colosseum, built by Emperor Vespasian in the first century A.D. to hold 80,000 spectators for gladiatorial fights. Enough of the ruins remain to see rows of stone seats for spectators and the basement cells where the lions were kept.

Our evening entertainment was at a hillside nightclub overlooking Rome. It was very romantic: a full moon, tables under palm trees, and mandolins playing. An Italian asked me to dance, and I was able to follow him as he led me through a samba, a mambo, and a tango – all very exotic for a Nebraskan.

Love, Fauneil

* * *

Dear Marleen,

Today our bus took us to Milan in northern Italy, where we toured the La Scala Opera House, one of the most beautiful, luxurious, and famous in Europe. Our next stop was the Cathedral of Milan. Its three stained-glass windows in the front are the largest in the world – 70 by 20 feet each. To me, this cathedral is the most beautiful of any we have seen. We next drove to a gallery where we saw Leonardo da Vince's painting, "The Last Supper." It was in poor condition, but still touchingly expressive.

Back to the bus, we headed for Geneva, Switzerland via the Simplon Pass over the Alps – breathtaking! The next day we visited the headquarters of the United Nations. The gardens were spectacular: brilliant flowers, cedar trees from Lebanon, and a huge gold revolving ball symbolizing the world.

I hope you are enjoying the summer, swimming, practicing music, and dating Carlton (Cartie).

Love, Fauneil

*   *   *

Letter to Lisetta and Walter   August 2, 1956

Dear Mom and Dad,

Today we went to Versailles, which is not far from Paris, to tour the palace built by King Louis XIV, who ruled France for 72 years. He was extremely self-centered. He had 40 servants to dress him; he changed wigs 15 times a day, choosing from among his 300 wigs; he had hundreds of high-heeled shoes, starting the fashion of high-heels (he was a very short and vain person). His huge palace had hundreds of rooms, including the Hall of Mirrors, with one wall lined with mirrors, framed in gold leaf, and crystal chandeliers, whose many candles took servants many hours to light prior to a ball.

He was succeeded by Louis XV and then by Louis XVI and his wife, Marie Antoinette, who were beheaded by guillotine during the French Revolution. While still living an opulent lifestyle at the palace, Marie often escaped from court life to the woods where she enjoyed her English-style thatched cottage, surrounded by gardens, a lily pond, and a windmill – which reminded me of Grandma's farm.

I wanted to go to the Eiffel Tower, but none of our group could accompany me, so I tried to find it by taking the subway. Unfortunately, my French wasn't good enough to get me there. The Parisiennes are not eager to help American tourists. C'est la Vie.

Love, Fauneil

*   *   *

Letter to Jeannine   August 3 & 4, 1956

Dear Jeannine,

In the morning, we took a sightseeing tour of Paris by bus, passing the Place de la Concorde, the Arche de Triomphe, Alexander's Bridge, the Church of Madeleine, the Eiffel Tower, and Napoleon's Tomb. In the afternoon, we visited the Louvre, a huge art museum. Among its treasures, we saw "The Mona Lisa" by Leonardo da Vinci and a statue of "Venus de Milo" circa 300 B.C.

In the evening, we all went to the Folies Bergere. The costumes were great but very skimpy. I'm sure the boys loved it. After that, Eileen and I hired a guide to take us night-clubbing. He picked us up in a limousine and drove us to a club, waited for us to enjoy it, and drove to the next. We saw a stage show at some, and each had a band and dance floor. We returned to our hotel at 5:00 AM., having been to the Moulin Rouge, the Lido, Pigalle, and the Latin Quarter. Along the way, several guys from West Point joined us. They made good dance partners. We ended the evening exhausted but elated!

Love, Fauneil

*   *   *

Letter to Lisetta and Walter   August 6 & 7, 1956

Dear Mom and Dad,

We are still in Paris. The day started by bus, which took us past the Sorbonne, the Sacre-Coeur, and Montmartre, where we stopped to shop for gifts. I got something for you! Then we toured the Notre Dame Cathedral, with its flying buttresses and its three rose stained-glass windows. In the afternoon, a boat ride on the Seine led us past many of the sights we had visited. It was interesting and beautiful to see Notre Dame again from the outside, especially the flying buttresses, which were built to hold up the walls of the Gothic structure.

In the evening, we went to the Opera House, which is huge and lavish. For the performance of Gounod's "Romeo and Juliet," we had seats in one of the lower balconies, which were ideal for good vision and hearing. The music was heavenly! It was the last performance before we head to our ship, the Castel Felice, which is waiting for us at Le Havre.

Our final day in Paris we spent on a walking tour to the Garden of the Tuileries, the Place de la Concorde, and the Champs Elysees, where we visited a "parfumerie" and got to sniff different fragrances. My favorite was Chanel #5.

After dinner, I packed. Tomorrow it's "Goodbye, Paris. I hope to see you again."

Love, Fauneil

* * *

Dear Grandma,

I am writing this on the bus from Paris to Le Havre, where our ship is waiting for us. It has been a wonderful trip to Europe. On board the ship, I will need to get busy writing a paper about a country of my choice. I will write about Germany because it is the country of your ancestors and mine.

It will take us nine days to cross the ocean and another two days on the train before I am home. I will post this just before we board the ship, so you should get it before I see you again.

Auf Wiedersehen, Fauneil

*   *   *

Chapter XVI
Reflections

Fauneil's train ride to South Dakota from New York City lasted 2 ½ days and two nights. She could afford only a coach seat, making the trip uncomfortable and tedious. She caught short naps rather than a good night's sleep. During her waking hours, she enjoyed the scenery, having never visited the states of New York, Pennsylvania, Ohio, and Illinois. Although she was soon again in the Midwest, her thoughts were still of Europe.

She reread her little red diary, and as she went from entry to entry, she reflected upon all that she had experienced and seen during the summer. She realized that before the trip, she had been a naïve twenty-year-old American girl; now she was a young woman, who had traveled to Europe, had gained first-hand knowledge, which was not attainable in books, had learned to appreciate other cultures and people, and had a better understanding of art, geography, and history.

 As a small-town Midwesterner, the largest city she had experienced was Omaha, Nebraska. Now she had visited the metropolises of London, Paris, and Rome. She had never been to a famous museum, gallery, cathedral, or castle. She had known nothing about oil paintings, statuary, murals, frescoes, tapestries, mosaics, or antiques. Huge cathedrals, with their stained-glass windows, high vaulted ceilings, and flying buttresses, amazed her. She had not understood the difference between Romanesque, Gothic, Byzantine, and Elizabethan architecture. She had not had explained to her the styles of the Baroque, Rococo, Classical, or Neo-classical periods.

Unlike the farmland in Nebraska, the scenery seemed to be ever changing: from farmland with hedge-rows to formal gardens, forests, majestic mountains with lakes and meadows, fjords, canals, islands, and ocean beaches. She had never crossed big bodies of water: the English Channel, the North Sea, the Adriatic Sea, the Mediterranean, or the Atlantic Ocean. She had traveled by boat, ocean liner, funicular, train, and a double-decker bus. She enjoyed, for the first time, an opera, a ballet, a puppet show, a concert with ancient instruments, and a night club show. She had tasted cuisine from cultures of eleven countries and was no longer familiar with only German and American food. She had been introduced to champagne and a variety of wines and beers.

Her knowledge of geography had widened. She could visualize each country and its borders with its neighbors. She understood how the Alps wound through Austria and Switzerland and touched France, Germany, and Italy. She enjoyed a cruise on a fjord in Norway, one on the Rhine River in Germany, another on the Seine in Paris, each with its different scenic views from the boat. She experienced the summer weather in each country and its relationship to location. She could visualize where the major cities and the smaller towns were situated in each country.

She learned about the history of Europe by seeing structures from different periods of time: the medieval buildings in Bavaria, the ruins and still-used aqueducts, cobble-stone roads, walls, and bridges built by the Romans; the cathedrals dating back to William the Conqueror, and the cottages and structures from Elizabethan times in England; and the Viking ships still recognizable in Norway.

Fauneil could now better understand World War II from the European point of view rather than from an American one. The rubble was still there to see in cities like London and Berlin. Some churches and other buildings partially remained in their bombed-out state and would not be rebuilt but left as a reminder of the devastating conflict between the Allies and the Axis. Fauneil was thankful that she and her family had lived in America, where no civilian lives had been lost, in contrast to thousands in some of the European countries and millions in others.

Because the study tour was intended to be a joyful time for members of the group, there was no visit to any of the concentration camps. However, lectures by Mr. and Mrs. Hartman, the tour guides, included details of the holocaust.

*   *   *

When Fauneil arrived in Yankton, South Dakota, Walter, Lisetta, and Jeannine were there to meet her. They were full of questions throughout the seventy-mile drive to Norfolk. When they arrived at 1208 Nebraska Avenue, Minnie was waiting on the porch. She had picked strawberries from her garden and had baked an angel food cake, using the whites from a dozen eggs that she had gathered from her hen house. She had frosted the cake with butter-cream frosting and had decorated it with twenty-one candles for Fauneil's birthday.

"You never forget a birthday, do you, Grandma?" Minnie smiled.

"Well, Fauneil, your birthday isn't until the 25th, but you'll be alone in Tucson. Why do you want to go so far away?"

"It's not as far as Europe was."

"What's next?" asked Walter. "The moon?"

*   *   *

Fauneil had only a few days to unpack her suitcase, distribute the gifts she had brought from Europe, and pack her entire wardrobe for Tucson. This time only Walter and Lisetta drove Fauneil to the train station. Jeannine was at home with her baby, David. Marleen was taking advantage of the last of the summer days to be with her boyfriend, Cartie. As Fauneil stepped into the coach of the train, Walter reminded her to write. "Often," added Lisetta. They waited until the train began to pull away and then waved goodbye.

"I don't know why Fauneil has to go off to some desert and live among cactuses instead of our green fields and meadows," grumbled Walter. "It almost breaks my heart."

"She's a pioneer, Walt, the first in the family to go to Europe and the first to move to the desert. Remember our ancestors, Walt. They came here as humble pioneers, and now Nebraska honors them for their spirit of adventure and bravery. Fauneil has that spirit, too."

*   *   *

As Fauneil sat in her seat on the train and watched the green landscape outside, she was wondering what living in a desert terrain would be like. She had just traveled from an area of Europe that her great grandparents had come from. They had crossed the Atlantic Ocean, taken a train to Illinois, and then joined a wagon train headed for the prairie. Norfolk and the surrounding communities had been settled by those early pioneers.

Minnie's generation had seen the horses and oxen replaced by local trains and early automobiles. The ambitious farmers among them had bought more land to add to their original homesteads; they had built sturdy wooden houses, barns, fences, and windmills and had increased their numbers of livestock.

Walter's and Lisetta's generation had experienced the thriving community that had been established by the previous generation, but then the Great Depression hit, followed by World War II. Because of their sacrifice and fortitude in these times of disaster, their generation had earned the title of "The Greatest Generation."

As an adult, a new era was beginning for Fauneil. She remembered starting school when all eight grades were taught in the same classroom by one teacher. Fauneil had been the only pupil in her grade and had learned mainly by listening to the upper grades. *How different schools have become*, she mused. She would attend a week of orientation for new teachers in a few days. Then she would step into **her** classroom! She was ready!

*   *   *

Chapter XVII
Letters to Fauneil from Lisetta

November 28, 1963

Dear Fauneil,

Now that Thanksgiving is over, I finally have time to write. Thanksgiving dinner was at our house this year. It seemed like all we could talk about at the dinner table was President Kennedy's assassination. I thought about you on the 22nd. You must have been teaching when the president was hit.

Fauneil, I worry about your returning to teaching less than a year following your chemotherapy. I hope you aren't asking your body to do too much too soon.

Dad and I are looking forward to our trip to the West Coast at Christmastime. I'll bring along pictures of baby Heather. She looks a lot like Holly did at that age. Lyla had a girl, born on the same day as Heather. Grandmother Meritz was written up in the paper as having been blessed with two great granddaughters on the same day. By the way, is my little namesake, Lise, potty trained yet?

Love, Mom

*   *   *

Dear Fauneil,   *April 30th, 1964*

As you requested, we included your name on the family bouquet for Aunt Lisetta. There were quite a few bouquets, but the funeral was attended mainly by members of the family. Aunt Lisetta died penniless. There was no will, but she left a note saying that her diamond ring, her only possession of value, should be given to Lise. She was so proud of her namesake, as I am.

Dad has his real estate and insurance businesses up for sale. He will retire from everything except his farm management. We are planning a trip to Europe in late August, returning in October. We have decided against joining a group tour. Dad kept all of the films, notes, letters, and the itinerary from your trip in 1956, and he feels that if we use your material as a guide, we can do it on our own. Since most Europeans can speak English fairly well, and we can speak German, we should be able to communicate throughout most of Europe. We will write you along the way. After all, sending letters was one of Dad's requests when you took your trip.

                                     Love, Mom

*   *   *

Dear Fauneil,   *August 2, 1965*

We have two new babies in the family: Jeannine and Ralph had a boy, Jonathan (their 4th child) on July 5th, and Marleen and Cartie had their first, Christine, not long after that. Jeannine and Ralph are living in Minneapolis, where Ralph works with Honeywell as an accountant. Marleen and Cartie are now in Norfolk, not far from 1208 Nebraska Ave. Cartie is an intern at the mortuary. Do you have their addresses?

Dad just returned home from a Lutheran Hospital Board meeting. He's glad he was in Norfolk for this. The administrator of the hospital has been at loggerheads with Doctor Brauer and was "out to get him" this evening. Dad and Lyle went to bat for Dr. Brauer and convinced the board to fire the administrator instead. With all that Dr. Brauer has done for our family throughout the years, he deserved a good turn.

Dad has asked me to relay that 1966 will be the centennial for St. Paul's Lutheran Church and for the city of Norfolk, as well. He is working hard as a member of the centennial committee. He says that it will be worth coming home for. I know it is early, but please think about plans for next summer.

Love, Mom

*   *   *

Dear Fauneil,   *August 25, 1966*

I hope that you, Tony, and Lise enjoyed the centennial celebrations in Norfolk this summer. Dad looked so handsome dressed up as a pioneer. I am glad that you saw our new house in the building stage. Do you like the location on 18th Street? Dad chose it so that he could watch the city lights from our living room at night. He plans to put in a large, sloping lawn and a rose garden at the back of the house. We have both agreed on plans for the inside. The living room will be large enough for the parlor grand piano, which will stay in the family.

Grandma is ready to leave the farm and looking forward to living at 1208 Nebraska Avenue again. She should be in the house by Christmastime. It will be good for me to have her close. Doctor Davidson, an associate of Dr. Brauer's, says that her heart muscle is weak, which explains her shortness of breath. He has put her on digitalis. Grandma still has a lot of spirit left, but she has failed dreadfully, and I don't know how long she will be with us. Keep her in your prayers.

Love, Mom

*   *   *

Dear Fauneil,   January 26, 1967

 Grandma fainted last week. She fell off the kitchen chair and lay there from fifteen to thirty minutes. Then she got up and called me. I thought it might have been a slight stroke, but Dr. Davidson said <u>no</u>. Several days later, she fainted again. This time she was taken to the emergency ward at the Lutheran Hospital.

She is out of danger, but she has to stay in the hospital until she is stronger. She has a room of her own in the southwest corner of the building. When she looks out of *her window, she can see the backyard of 1208 Nebraska Avenue. At first Grandma was too weak to move out of bed, but for   the last few days, they have gotten her up to sit in a chair for several hours, for the sake of circulation in her limbs.*

I have been spending most of my time with her, but Doctor Davidson has asked me to be there less so that she becomes more dependent on the nurses and less on her family. He doesn't seem to understand what an independent woman Grandma is.

 I am taking it one day at a time and have accepted whatever will be the Lord's way. Please write to Grandma. She would love to hear from you.

Love, Mom
*   *   *

Dear Fauneil,   *June 30, 1967*

I know you will be glad to hear about Grandma. She has surprised us all with her recuperation. For months, she has felt capable of moving back to 1208 Nebraska, and now Doctor Davidson has agreed to it. I am still going over to her house each day to see her and spend time with her.

Dad has been restless lately. He says there's nothing to do around here. It's a big lot to keep up, but not big enough for him. He's talking about finding himself a retirement project, an acreage perhaps – somewhere where he can spend all day   puttering around outside, pretending that he's on a farm again.

By the way, Marleen has had her second baby, Gregory. She and Cartie are living in Lincoln, where Cartie has a job as a mortician. Do you have their address?

Love, Mom

*   *   *

P.S. Lise, how are your piano and ballet lessons going? Do you like to practice? Your mommy always did when she was a little girl.

*   *   *

Dear Fauneil,   *March 15th, 1968*

We were glad to hear that Tony's open- heart surgery went well and that he is finally able to return to work. Three months is a long time to be an invalid, and it must have been hard on you, Fauneil, to keep up with school, house, garden, a daughter, and a husband in poor health.

Grandma is doing well. On April 14th, at Easter this year, we will celebrate her 83rd birthday. She would like all of her family to be together, but we know that won't be possible. Write her a letter. It would mean so much to her.

Dad has been as busy as a beaver with the eighty acres he purchased south of Norfolk. He's hired a man to come out with his bulldozer and move around dirt to create three man-made lakes instead of the swampy ground that is there. He plans to name the lakes after his three oldest granddaughters: Holly, Heather, and Lise. When that is done, he will create a residential area and begin building houses. He comes home as cheerful as a meadow lark after he's been out there working in the dirt all day.

Love, Mom

P.S. Lise, I understand you have a kitty named Puffy. I'll bet he's cute. Write and tell us all about him.

* * *

Dear Fauneil,   June 20, 1969

Grandma is still at 1208. We got her a cane, and she is getting along remarkably well for her age. When I stopped by to see her yesterday, she was out behind the garage pulling weeds – without her cane – still **independent!** I couldn't believe it.

Dad and I have decided to sell our house on 18th St. and build a house on the acreage he purchased. It is so pretty out there now with the lakes and the trees that Dad has planted. He has stocked the lakes with fish and is looking forward to fishing when they are big enough.

You know, all of those years when you girls were growing up, we lived in houses we didn't own. I was never quite satisfied, always wanting our own home. Then Dad and I planned and built a brick house to suit us. But Dad has felt

155

confined here, and I have found that I don't need this house to be happy. It will be good to get back to the countryside.

Love, Mom

* * *

Chapter XVIII
The Birthday Party

On August 16, 1969, Lyle Meritz turned sixty. A celebration with Minnie and his four children and their families was held in his honor at his farm, which Lyle had inherited from Gus and Minnie. Two weeks later, Lyle and Marcella hosted a small dinner party, with Oliver and Loretta, and Walter and Lisetta, to celebrate Lisetta's 57th birthday on August 31st.

As Walter and Lisetta drove into the farmyard, they were impressed with how prosperous and carefully tended the farm looked. After the Great Depression, Lyle had added a dairy operation to supplement his income from corn crops and livestock. Walter commented to Lisetta about the tall metal containers for storage and the large cow barn with its automated machines for milking the cows.

Lisetta responded with positive comments about the house, which had been her home from age three until early childhood. It had been well-built by Gus and Minnie and had retained its stolid, attractive appearance.

Prior to dinner, the company were served wine in the living room. The conversation centered around family news.

Lyle addressed Walter. "Where are your daughters living now?"

"Jeannine is in San Diego, Fauneil is in San Jose, and Marleen is in Lincoln."

"Two in California then," responded Lyle. "Ours are closer to home. Lyla and Lon are in Norfolk, and Lane is on Mother's farm, across the road."

"And Loy? Has he graduated from the U?" asked Lisetta.

Marcella responded. "He graduated in May and is in officers' training school in the army. When he is finished, he will be sent to Vietnam. I'm just **sick** about it."

When the party moved into the dining room, Marcella served a pork roast with mashed potatoes and gravy, corn-on-the-cob, peas from the garden, coleslaw, and peach pie for dessert.

The conversation about Vietnam continued: "I don't understand what we're doing there," said Marcella. "What kind of country is it!" Oliver, who had been interested in history since his university days, attempted to answer her question:

"Vietnam was controlled by China and then won its independence in the early 1400s. It was governed locally by mandarins. Unrest caused a civil war to break out, which divided Vietnam between the north and the south.

"In the early 1800s, Gia Long became the emperor and unified the country. That lasted for close to fifty years.

During the 19th century, the French took over Vietnam, as well as Cambodia, calling the area Indochina. They made it a protectorate of France and then a colony. That's why French is spoken in Vietnam.

"In the 1930s, the Indochinese communist party began to gain control. After World War II, in 1950 Ho Chi Minh, the communist leader, declared that the Democratic Republic of Vietnam was the only *legal* government in the country."

"A democracy?" asked Lisetta.

"No, the word *democratic* is misleading. It is a *communis*t regime."

"So that's why the U.S. got involved – the fight between East and West, between communism and democracy," explained Lyle.

"It didn't happen immediately," said Oliver. "SEATO was formed to stem communism. It stands for Southeast Asia Treaty Organization and includes (*here Oliver counted the countries on his fingers*) the U.S., Britain, Australia, New Zealand, Pakistan, Thailand, and the Philippines."

"What about the U.S.S.R. and China?" asked Walter. "They're in the Southeast."

"They recognized the *communist* republic as the *legal* one. By this time, there were two republics: the communist North Vietnam Republic and the non-communist South Vietnam Republic."

"So how exactly did the U.S. get involved in the war?" asked Lisetta.

"It was a gradual involvement," answered Oliver. "The U.S. first funneled aid to the government in Saigon in 1955 and then agreed   to train the South Vietnamese army. When North Vietnam began sending weapons into South Vietnam via the Ho Chi Minh Trail (which, to a large extent, runs through neighboring Laos), the U.S. responded with military assistance to South Vietnam.

"In 1965, the Vietcong Army attacked American installations; the U.S. sent more of our troops – 400,000 by the end of 1966. The   Vietcong responded with the Tet offensive: Twenty-three major battles were fought throughout North and South Vietnam. One of the bloodiest was in Hue, where there was house- to- house fighting. Both sides had heavy casualties."

"Oliver, you said *Tet*. What does that mean?" asked Marcella.

"It stands for the Vietnamese lunar New Year. The Vietcong offensive began on January 31st."

"Who knows how long this will go on," complained Marcella.

"Perhaps it will all be over by the time Loy gets there, like it was for my brother Hank in World War I," said Walter.

"I don't know," responded Lyle. "Remember what happened in the Korean War. Peace talks continued for several years after the major fighting stopped, but skirmishes continued until an agreement was signed."

"It's impossible to know what political influence Washington will continue to have. Our leaders are so divided and indecisive," commented Loretta.

"Yes," agreed Lisetta. "And the American public are becoming more and more dissatisfied. Look at the number of anti-war demonstrations!"

"Heaven only knows!" added Walter. "If the Vietcong continue to suffer heavy bombing casualties and *still* have the *determination* and *bravery* to fight on, they will win. We will give up, not for lack of *power*, but for lack of *will*."

"Unfortunately, I agree," concluded Oliver.

* * *

When Walter and Lisetta got home, Walter, who had been impressed by Oliver's knowledge, began to research information about the conflict that the U. S. was engaging in. He continued staying informed throughout the coming years, until the U.S. pulled out of the war, allowing communist control of Vietnam.

War News
Vietnam, 1969 – 1975

March 18, 1969   -   President Nixon begins secret bombing of communist sanctuaries in Cambodia.

September 3, 1969   -   Ho Chi Minh, the Communion leader, dies.

October 15, 1969   -   Massive anti-war demonstrations are held in Washington.

December, 1969   -   American troop strength is reduced by 60,000.

May 4, 1970   -   Large anti-war protests spread across the U.S., including at Kent State University, where four students are killed.

November 12, 1970   -   Lieutenant Calley goes on trial for his part in the Mylai massacre of Vietnamese peasants.

December, 197   -   American troop strength is reduced to 140,000.

January 25, 1972   -   President Nixon reveals that Henry Kissinger had been negotiating secretly with the North Vietnamese.

January 27, 1973   -   Cease-fire agreements are formally signed in Paris.

*January, 1974   -   Nguyen Van Thieu, President of South Vietnam, declares that war had resumed.

*August, 1974   -   President Nixon resigns to avoid impeachment. His last act as president is to sign into law a bill that imposed a ceiling of $1,000,000,000 on U. S. aid to South Vietnam for eleven months.

*April 30, 1975   -   Communist forces capture Saigon. North and   South Vietnam are now controlled by a communist government. President Thieu leaves Saigon for a residence in Taiwan.

Notes:

1. The cost of the Vietnam War from 1955 – 1975 added greatly to the U.S. debt. (By 1989, the U.S. had become the world's largest debtor nation.)
2. The Vietnam War was the longest undeclared war in U.S. history.
3. Out of 3,000,000 Americans who served, 58,000 were killed. 4,000,000 Vietnamese soldiers and civilians perished (10% of the population.)
4. The post-war exodus of Vietnamese was the biggest migration in modern times.
5. The U.S. entered the war with an attitude of American exceptionalism and a desire to transform the Vietnam nation into a democracy.
6. The American public's approval lessoned with the continual weakness shown by the South Vietnamese leadership and its army.

7. *The American soldiers misunderstood the military tactics of the Vietcong and distrusted the peasants, who sided with either North or South.*
8. *The U.S. public approval for the war gradually changed by television, which carried the violence into American homes, the news commentators, and the anti-war demonstrations.*
9. *Although the U.S. had superior military power, the North Vietnamese had the tenacity, aggressiveness, wiliness, and bravery to win.*

At the dinner party in 1969, Walter was prescient when he said, "We will give up, not for lack of power, but for lack of will.

*   *   *

Chapter XIX, 1969
Minnie

When Fauneil answered the telephone at 5:00 in the afternoon on Sunday, November 16th, she heard her mother's voice.

"Fauneil?"

"Yes. Hello Mom."

"Grandma Meritz died. We found her at noon."

"Oh, no!"

"Her funeral will be on Wednesday. Can you come?"

"Yes. I can get bereavement leave from school, and I'll bring Lise with me. I don't think that Tony will be able to come, though."

"That's alright. Let us know what your flight plans are, and we'll drive to Omaha to get you."

"Okay. How did Grandma die, Mom?"

"I'll tell you about it on the way home from Omaha. We'll have plenty of time to visit then. Bring warm clothes. It's cold here."

*　　*　　*

The following day, they visited in the car en route to Norfolk:

"We're not sure how or when Grandma died," said Lisetta. "When I stopped over to see her on Saturday, she seemed to be fine. She was looking forward to a get-together at Lyle's the next day. Loy is leaving for Vietnam soon, and Grandma was anxious to see him. She told me that she was planning to take an angel food cake for the occasion. I asked her if she wanted me to pick her up for church in the morning. She said *no; she was a little tired. It would be a long day, and she would just rest in the morning*.

"On Sunday morning, Dad and I went to church. Afterwards we stopped at our house to get a casserole, which I had prepared to take to Lyle's. Then we drove to 1208 Nebraska to pick up Grandma.

"When she didn't answer the door, I knew something was wrong. I had my key with me, but the storm door was locked from the inside, and we couldn't get in. Dad and I walked around to the side of the house and looked into her bedroom window. We could see that her bedside lamp was still burning.

"Dad went across the street to Clanton's Grocery and got a screwdriver. He pried off a storm window, climbed through, and unlocked the door for me. We called. No answer. In the bedroom, we could see that Grandma's bed was unmade. Then Dad walked down the hall to the bathroom and found her lying there. 'Don't go in there,' he said. 'I'm going to call Doctor Davidson.' While he was on the phone, I went in anyway. I wanted to see for myself. She was lying with her head propped up against the wall and her neck and limbs bent in a funny way as though she had fallen and hadn't had time to straighten herself out. She had one slipper on and one slipper off, and her cane was lying close by. She had skinned the top of her nose. It looked as though she may have grabbed onto the sink as she fell."

"What did Doctor Davidson say when he examined her?" asked Fauneil.

"He said that she had died a sudden death, and that she had been dead for some time. You see, we found her at noon, and her bedside light was still burning, so she must have gotten up at night to go to the bathroom. "After they had taken Grandma out, I went through the house to see if everything was locked up. When I went into the kitchen, there sat her angel food cake with butter-cream frosting. That's when I burst into tears."

"What a great lady Grandma was!" exclaimed Fauneil. "Her last effort was to please the family. She knew how much we all enjoyed her angel food cake."

Lisetta paused, wiped her eyes, and blew into her handkerchief. "Speaking of cake, I have one at home for you, Lise. What a way to spend a birthday when you're eight years old."

"That's alright, Grandma."

"We'll try to celebrate your birthday a little tonight. You'll have some presents to open."

The next day, Lisetta and Walter and their family went to the mortuary to view Minnie's body. Minnie looked the way she had always looked when she dressed for important occasions. She was wearing her black dress, her gold beads, and her gold wedding band. Her hair was parted in the middle and waved just enough to keep her from looking severe.

The following morning was the funeral at St. Paul's. The church was filled with friends and relatives from Norfolk, Hoskins, and places farther away. Lisetta saw Minnie's lifelong friend, Minnie Krause, in the congregation. She remembered the two Minnies whispering to each other in German on the street in Norfolk during World War I, when German became a forbidden language.

The service began with the hymn, "Nearer My God to Thee," which had been sung at Gus's funeral when Lisetta was fifteen and Minnie was forty-three. Lisetta still felt the pang of her father's death, but she felt blessed that Minnie had held the family together without bitterness or self-pity for forty-one years.

Following the service, the congregation proceeded to the burial site at Prospect Hill Cemetery. The large granite headstone that Minnie had purchased for Gus's grave was engraved with his name and dates: *Gustave Julius Meritz,*

1883 – 1928. The dates for Minnie would soon be engraved next to her name: Minnie Emilie Meritz, 1885 – 1969.

As the family gathered around the gravesite, Lisetta's eyes dropped to the ground. Close to the open grave, some stubborn blades of grass were still green. Since summer, the frost had come and gone several times already, and a layer of snow blanketed the ground, with these stubborn sprigs just peeking through. Among them was a dandelion, whose flower had turned to seeds that had not yet blown away. Lisetta recalled the time when she was a little girl, and she and Hank had sat on the prairie grass to have a piece of Minnie's *Kaffeekuchen*. Hank had pulled up a plant called a shooting star, whose flower had turned to seeds. "Watch," he said, blowing the seeds. "Some of these are being carried away by the wind. And some of them have fallen here into the grass. They'll stay here all through the winter, safe and warm, and next spring beautiful new stars will shoot up out of the earth."

THE END

Looking back:

In writing the book, I wanted to show what daily life was like for Walter and Lisetta's family from 1938 – 1969. During that time, the U. S. was involved in three wars. All of the characters in the story were aware of the effects of war. For the adults, the current war sometimes caused fear, worry, or sorrow. At other times, war was on the periphery of their thoughts. For the children, World War II was a source of play.

Minnie had lost her brother Ernest in World War I. When Hank was drafted for World War II, he left the farm, and Minnie lost her best farm worker. During World War II, Walter was afraid that his family would suffer financially if he was called to serve. His flat feet saved him, while four of his nephews saw action. During The Korean War, his nephew Howard lost his life fighting in Korea. Walter and Lisetta experienced sorrow for Hank and his wife Tillie, who grieved over the loss of their son. As the story ends, Lyle and his wife Marcella are worried that Loy, their youngest son, will be killed in Vietnam.

These Mid-westerners were Christians, who believed that God was ultimately in control, but that man's nature was subject to conflict. As Lisetta quoted from the Bible at the dinner party: *"There will be wars and rumors of wars until the end of the earth."*

Bibliographical sources for the wars:

The definitive Visual Guide   by The Smithsonian

The Korean War, A History   by Bruce Cumings

Vietnam, A History   by Stanley Karnow